5-INGREDIENT
VEGAN

Also by Nava Atlas

COOKBOOKS

Plant Power
Wild About Greens
Vegan Holiday Kitchen
Vegan Soups and Hearty Stews for All Seasons
Vegan Express
The Vegetarian Family Cookbook
The Vegetarian 5-Ingredient Gourmet
Great American Vegetarian
Vegetarian Express
Vegetarian Celebrations
Vegetariana

VISUAL NONFICTION

The Literary Ladies' Guide to the Writing Life
Secret Recipes for the Modern Wife
Expect the Unexpected When You're Expecting! (A Parody)

5-INGREDIENT VEGAN

175

SIMPLE, PLANT-BASED RECIPES FOR
DELICIOUS, HEALTHY MEALS IN MINUTES

NAVA ATLAS

STERLING EPICURE
New York

STERLING EPICURE
New York

An Imprint of Sterling Publishing Co., Inc.
1166 Avenue of the Americas
New York, NY 10036

ISBN 978-1-4549-3355-7

Distributed in Canada by Sterling Publishing Co., Inc.
c/o Canadian Manda Group, 664 Annette Street
Toronto, Ontario M6S 2C8, Canada
Distributed in the United Kingdom by GMC Distribution Services
Castle Place, 166 High Street, Lewes, East Sussex BN7 1XU, England
Distributed in Australia by NewSouth Books
University of New South Wales, Sydney, NSW 2052, Australia

For information about custom editions, special sales, and premium
and corporate purchases, please contact Sterling Special Sales
at 800-805-5489 or specialsales@sterlingpublishing.com.

Manufactured in China

2 4 6 8 10 9 7 5 3 1

sterlingpublishing.com

Cover design by Elizabeth Lindy
Interior design by Christine Heun
Photography credits on page 212

CONTENTS

INTRODUCTION

As a longtime vegan, it has been incredible to watch this way of eating and living grow from a trend to a mainstay. Vegan options are blossoming from urban centers to country corners, staking a permanent place in the culinary landscape.

Case in point: Back in the 1980s, my husband and I—vegetarians at the time—took a driving tour of the southern United States and found it challenging to find a decent meal. Vegan wasn't even on the radar. Fast-forward to 2017, when I visited the Nashville area. Since I was staying in a place with a kitchenette, I was delighted to find well-stocked vegan sections in every supermarket where I shopped for supplies. Even in the land of barbecue, vegan eateries are now abundant! And on a recent visit to Iceland—not only in Reykjavik but in remote outposts—I found a veritable paradise of vegan options. I could go on, but that old question, "Don't you have trouble eating out as a vegan?" now has a one-word answer: "No."

The concepts of "vegan" and "plant-based" are now firmly woven into the food vocabulary nearly everywhere. As wonderful as it is to travel and discover a growing vegan world, let's turn our attention back to our own kitchens. Many people tell me they'd like to enjoy more vegan meals at home, and that's exactly what this book aims to encourage and make as easy as possible. There's still a stubborn perception of plant-based meals being time-consuming, complicated, expensive, and filled with esoteric ingredients. It doesn't have to be that way, and honestly, it usually isn't.

Since I'm a prolific cookbook author, no one believes me when I confess how lazy I've become in the kitchen. Meals that take thirty minutes or less to prepare have always been my preference, but now they're practically a must. I still do love to cook, but life has become crowded. I think this is true for most people I know. Gone are the days, for whatever reason, when we can noodle around in the kitchen for a couple of hours, a glass of wine in hand.

Some years ago, when my family and I were still vegetarians (the concept of vegan was just coming on the radar), I wrote a book called *The Vegetarian 5-Ingredient Gourmet*. Trust me, the word "gourmet" was used very loosely! It wasn't one of my best or prettiest books—there's not a single photo in it—but it was one of my best-selling works. The reason is that it focused on ease and simplicity. To reiterate the book's basic premise, simplicity doesn't imply mindlessness, but rather echoes Walt Whitman's view that "Simplicity is the glory of expression." With a few well-chosen ingredients, a simple meal can be as delicious as a more elaborate one. And now, since vegan cooking is so popular, I decided to write another 5-ingredient cookbook, this one specifically for vegans, in which simplicity is key.

Simple recipes can be used as templates to build upon or embellish. I encourage you to take your favorites from this book and make them your own by adding or substituting ingredients you have on hand. Simple recipes are almost impossible to get "wrong." They don't demand the kind of precision and techniques of more complex preparations in order to taste great.

When only five ingredients are used, shortcuts are inevitable. I've always loved good-quality shortcuts, especially delicious ready-made sauces like teriyaki, peanut satay, marinara, salsa, and Indian simmer sauces. Stocking your pantry with them ensures that you're already partway to a tasty meal. The menu suggestions and pairings following many of the recipes show how to round out a meal. For the purposes of this book, the ingredients that don't "count" are salt, pepper, water, and cooking oil—the latter being because there are some oil-free folks for whom its use will be optional.

EASY DOES IT

I'm thinking of the many times I've heard someone stand in front of a painting in a gallery or museum and say, "My five-year-old could have done that." But your five-year-old didn't. Underlying that deceptively simple work of art that looks like anyone could have done it may be a great deal of thought and planning. That minimalist color field might contain big ideas about composition and balance. Besides, your kid didn't think to do it. Otherwise, museums would be filled with paintings by toddlers and children!

The same goes for certain recipes— well, kind of. Does anyone really need a cookbook to tell them to slather **Baked Tofu and Green Beans with Teriyaki Marinade** and serve it with store-bought sushi (as I've done on page 81)? For some people who desperately need ideas for meal plans, it could be a lifesaver. Maybe it's a frazzled parent just coming home after taking three kids to ballet and soccer practice. Or someone who, after a long day of work and a crazy commute, is tired of takeout. What often trips up busy people who have every intention of eating well is that daily dilemma of planning meals that are healthy, taste great, and can be on the table in half an hour or less. Super-simple recipes and meals need thought and care to make them tasty and healthy.

And that's what this book aims to do for you, whether you fall into the category of busy, lazy (which is okay, because evidently, your intentions are good!), or newly veg-curious. It's also for the solo cook. A large proportion of adults live on their own, and they may not be motivated to make anything beyond the most rudimentary meals. This book lets you feed yourself well—with the added benefit of leftovers.

Filled with suggestions on how to create a complete meal and tips on what dishes go well together, this book is here to help you get meals on the table that are fast and fun, not a daily ordeal. You might even think of this book as a kind of cousin to meal kits—but with meals that take a lot less time to make and minus the insane amount of packaging and waste. All this being said, the menu suggestions following many of the recipes aren't set in stone. Once you scope out your favorite recipes, feel free to mix and match—or just enjoy them on their own.

VEGAN 101

If you're just starting to explore veganism, here's a quick overview. What is a vegan (sometimes known as plant-based) diet, and how is it different from a vegetarian diet? Vegans avoid all animal products, including eggs, dairy products, and even honey. Vegetarians avoid meat, fowl, and seafood, and are often in it for the health aspects. Ethical veganism goes beyond diet—animal welfare is the top motivation for this designation. Concern for animal welfare means that any animal-derived products, including leather and wool, are avoided. Environmental issues weigh in as well.

As for food, the ideal vegan diet is based on fresh produce, whole grains, beans and other legumes, nuts, and seeds. Often in the mix are nondairy milks, soy foods, and, for some, meat and cheese alternatives. Even if you're not planning to go full-on vegan, anyone can benefit from enjoying plant-based meals on a regular basis. They're delicious and satisfying, and you just might feel more amazing than you ever thought possible.

GREAT REASONS TO GO VEGAN

Those who have embraced the vegan lifestyle appreciate knowing that their food choices can be not only tasty and healthful, but compassionate and humane as well. Choosing plant-based foods has been highlighted as a hopeful way to mitigate the alarming deterioration of the environment and increase food security. Here are some specific reasons to go vegan:

HEALTH: Research has shown that populations with primarily plant-based diets suffer from a fraction of the ailments that afflict meat eaters. These include heart disease, certain forms of cancer, and adult-onset (type 2) diabetes. Other benefits include:

* Studies have shown that eating foods high in fiber and complex carbohydrates can help reduce the risk of heart disease. In addition, plant-based proteins are more likely to reduce cholesterol levels, while animal protein raises them.

* Vegetarians, and especially vegans, tend to have lower overall rates of obesity,

not a small point to make at a time when 60% of American adults are overweight, with some 300,000 yearly deaths from obesity-related diseases, including hypertension, kidney disease, osteoporosis, and arthritis. A well-planned diet centered on whole grains, legumes, vegetables, and fruits provides a feeling of fullness that keeps the body fueled and satisfied for hours and staves off cravings for empty calories that lead to weight gain.

* Plant-based foods are less likely to cause virulent food-borne illnesses caused by *E. coli*, salmonella, and listeria. Children are especially vulnerable where food-borne illness is concerned, as their immune systems may not be developed enough to withstand the dangers of contaminated meat products. Note that this isn't foolproof, however. Some plant crops are contaminated from animal agriculture runoff, so it's important to pay attention to recalls no matter where you are on the dietary spectrum.

* If you're intrigued by the promise of longevity, studies conducted on Seventh-Day Adventists (who advocate a plant-based diet) have

shown that they typically live an average of 7 to 15 years longer than meat-eaters.

* Farmed animals are fed a steady diet of antibiotics and often hormones that have no place in their system, let alone yours. There have been many well-researched articles on how this practice can lead to antibiotic resistance in humans, and it's alarming.

ETHICS: For ethical vegans, the driving motivation is compassion toward all sentient beings. Animal agriculture often is unimaginably cruel. Each year, tens of millions of animals are confined, overcrowded, and disfigured. The human factor counts as well—slaughterhouse workers have one of the most dangerous and stressful jobs on the planet.

Some people wonder about dairy cows—after all, they "don't have to die." That may be true, but without going into the grueling details, mother cows have the toughest lot imaginable. If you want to learn more, films like *Peaceable Kingdom*, *Earthlings*, and *Vegucated* are eye-openers, and sometimes life-changers. And consider the fact that humans are the only species that drinks the milk of another species, and the only species that drinks milk after being weaned.

ENVIRONMENT: Getting most or all of your nutritional needs from plant-based foods means that you're "eating low on the food chain." Consider the following:

* Reducing the demand for animal products lessens the need for pesticides used to grow animal feed as well as antibiotic residues in the environment and in the food that's consumed by humans.

* The raising of livestock depletes enormous land and water resources and contributes to the loss of millions of tons of irreplaceable topsoil each year. It takes 25 gallons of water to produce a pound of wheat, as compared to 390 gallons of water to produce a pound of beef.

* Animal waste is a major pollutant for soil, water, and air.

* From the practical standpoint of food security, animal agribusiness cements a system that feeds those who already have enough to eat. Vast land resources are given over to grow grain used to feed animals—land that could be used to grow food for direct human consumption.

* Finally, a crucially important fact is that animal agriculture is a major

contributor to the greenhouse gases that lead to climate change. According to a groundbreaking 2006 report by the Food and Agriculture Organization (FAO) of the United Nations, the animal agriculture sector emits up to 18% of global, human-induced greenhouse gas emissions, and, according to the report, "mapping has shown a strong relationship between excessive nitrogen in the atmosphere and the location of intensive farm animal production areas." Deforestation for farm animal production has had devastating repercussions for the environment as well. Study after study has shown that animal agriculture is the second leading cause of greenhouse gases, not far behind fossil fuels.

If you're interested in the impact of animal agriculture on climate change, this concise, one-page report based on the FAO's finding can change your worldview: http://tinyurl.com/3hsh46c. While enjoying the tasty meals in the pages ahead, you can also feel good knowing that your food choices can help mitigate the climate crisis. In a world where effecting change is an enormous challenge, it's something every individual can do every day.

STOCKING UP FOR SIMPLE, HEALTHY MEALS

Keeping your pantry and refrigerator stocked up in a smart way goes a long way to solving the daily "What should I make for dinner?" dilemma. Here's a basic pantry list tailored to the meals in this book.

FRESH PRODUCE

Produce available only during a specific season is almost a thing of the past. Still, I prefer to use produce in its traditional season as much as possible, and the more local, the better, for optimal flavor and a smaller ecological footprint. Here's a basic list of what to keep on hand:

In the pantry
Garlic, onions, potatoes, sweet potatoes

On the countertop
Avocados that are ripening, bananas, tomatoes (including cherry or grape tomatoes)

In the vegetable drawer
You need not keep all of these at all times, but here are the veggies I find most useful and like to have on hand: Baby greens (spinach, arugula, "power greens"), bell peppers, broccoli, cabbage (green and/or red), and/or bagged coleslaw, carrots and/or baby carrots, cucumbers, kale, lettuce and/or mixed baby greens, scallions

Seasonal and occasional produce
Purchase these vegetables as needed: Asparagus, beets, brussels sprouts, celery, chard, collard greens, corn, eggplant, green beans, yellow summer squash, zucchini

In the fruit drawer
Apples, lemons, limes, oranges, pears

Seasonal and occasional fruit
Berries, melons, stone fruits

A WORD ABOUT ORGANIC PRODUCE

Is it important to use organic produce? In some cases, it sure is. It *is* slightly more expensive, but one way to save money while saving the earth is by consulting the Environmental Working Group's annual lists of the Dirty Dozen™ and Clean Fifteen™ produce. The Dirty Dozen are the fruits and vegetables that are grown with the most pesticides. Consumers would do well to buy the organic varieties of the produce on this list.

On the other hand, the Clean Fifteen list features fruits and vegetables that have little or no pesticide residue. That's where you can economize on your food budget, though you can always buy these in organic form as well if you choose. For information on EWG's annual lists, visit ewg.org/foodnews/dirty-dozen.php.

If there's an argument against organic produce, it's that it isn't necessarily more nutritious than conventionally grown. That may be true, but who needs to consume all those toxins? Pesticides also become part of the soil, groundwater, and air. And there's the human factor, which is rarely discussed. The fact that farmworkers who harvest pesticide-laden produce get sick at higher rates is rarely discussed.

CANNED, JARRED, AND PACKAGED PRODUCTS

Depending on usage and how much storage space you have, here are some products to consider keeping on hand. They're used regularly in this book.

BEANS: The varieties of beans most used in these pages are black, pinto, kidney, and cannellini beans, as well as chickpeas. I recommend organic canned beans, which are more flavorful and less salty. Look for BPA-free cans whenever possible. An

alternative to canned beans is beans packed in aseptic packages. Beans in this type of packaging, which is very similar to the kind of boxes that hold silken tofu, have so far made it into natural foods stores more so than supermarkets. These are a bit more ecological, though not more economical. If you cook your own beans, so much the better!

BOUILLON CUBES: Vegetable-based bouillon cubes infuse quick soups and cooked grains with extra flavor. Choose an all-natural brand, preferably a salt-free brand—best to control sodium content yourself.

COCONUT MILK: Keep a can or two on hand for use in noodle dishes, stews, and sauces. Light coconut milk is my preference—it tastes just as good but harbors a lot less fat.

INDIAN SIMMER SAUCES: I've always been too lazy to roast and grind and mix and measure the myriad spices that add up to the amazing flavors in Indian dishes. Indian simmer sauces, which are relatively new on the market, have been a game-changer for me. Look for them in the international foods aisles in supermarkets and natural foods stores.

Varieties come in a range of vegan options from mild to spicy, including Goan coconut, Kashmir curry, Jalfrezi, and Madras curry. Some of them include dairy, so cheßck labels. Some of the key ingredients in the vegan sauces are coconut milk, tomato, ginger, garlic, and, of course, lots of spices. Whatever you add these sauces to will take on the rich, complex flavors that can otherwise only be experienced at fine Indian restaurants.

LENTILS: Organic canned brown lentils are tasty and hold their shape nicely. I consider them a great time-saver because I never remember to cook lentils in advance of when I need them. Red lentils, however, cook quickly (15 to 20 minutes), so I do enjoy having them on hand as a soup base.

NONDAIRY MILK: Not long ago, the only varieties of nondairy milk were soy milk and rice milk. Now there's a range of options including almond, cashew, hemp, oat, and more. Many are available in refrigerated half-gallons, but the 32-ounce shelf-stable cartons keep for a long time in the pantry. Plain unsweetened varieties are the most useful for cooking; vanilla is nice for baking and using in cereals and smoothies.

NUTRITIONAL YEAST: For those who are new to "nooch" (as vegans have nicknamed nutritional yeast), don't confuse it with brewer's or baker's yeasts. Often described as having a somewhat fermented, cheese-y flavor, nutritional yeast is fortified with nutrients, especially B vitamins and potassium. Of special note to vegans is that it's a reliable source of B_{12}, a vitamin that's rare in plant foods.

VEGETABLE BROTH: For quick soups, a good vegetable broth can be a great starter. I find them especially useful in Asian-style soups. Look for all-natural ingredients with lots of herbs and seasonings and low sodium.

A FEW ONCE-IN-A-WHILE ITEMS

The recipes in this book use a few special (but not esoteric) ingredients for fun, variety, and concentrated flavor. These include marinated artichoke hearts, roasted red peppers, cured black olives, green pimiento olives, and sun-dried tomatoes. Stock your favorites regularly or buy as needed.

GRAINS

There are many great whole grains to incorporate into a whole-food, plant-based diet, but for the purposes of this book, I decided to keep it simple and use mainly brown rice (my favorite is Basmati) and quinoa, the staples I keep on hand at all times. You might like to expand your grain repertoire occasionally with farro, grits, barley, kasha, and others; purchase them as needed when they're part of your meal plans.

PASTA AND NOODLES

For Asian-style, Italian, and other pasta specialties, keep an assortment of varieties on hand. Some I find most useful are cavatappi, rotini, shells, and spaghetti. Whole-grain and gluten-free pasta varieties keep expanding and improving. Depending on how often you make Asian-style dishes, consider keeping soba (buckwheat noodles), udon, and rice vermicelli on hand, or purchase as needed.

FROZEN VEGETABLES

Flash-frozen vegetables can be as nutritious as their fresh counterparts, but with a few exceptions they're not as appealing. Since the window for really good, fresh green beans is so limited, I like frozen whole green beans (preferably organic). Green peas and corn kernels are quite useful. Cauliflower florets and riced cauliflower can come in handy as well.

CONDIMENTS

Ketchup and mustard are must-haves, of course, and need no explanation. Here are other condiments I find most useful to keep on hand:

BARBECUE SAUCE: Melding sweet, smoky, tangy, and spicy flavors, barbecue sauce goes a long way to boosting bean dishes, plant proteins, and roasted vegetables. Look for an all-natural brand without high-fructose corn syrup and other additives.

GINGER: The trouble with fresh ginger is that you never know if it will be fresh and moist, or dry and stringy. As a fan of ginger, I like to keep a squeezable bottle of it on hand. It's always good, and a nice time-saver when making quick meals. Look for it in the produce section of well-stocked supermarkets.

HOISIN SAUCE: Dense and fragrant, Hoisin sauce is a nice alternative to soy sauce in vegetable stir-fries and noodle dishes. Sweet, salty, and a bit pungent, you'll find it used in a number of recipes in this book.

LEMON AND/OR LIME JUICE: When you're out of fresh lemons and limes, it's nice to have lemon or lime juice in the fridge. Citrus is a friend to your digestive system, and as a flavor element, it reduces the need for salt.

MARINARA SAUCE: With so many wonderful choices on the market, purchase whatever pleases your palate—or what's on sale. As long as it's an all-natural brand that's not loaded with sugar or sodium, you have your choice of sauces highlighting herbs, garlic, wine, mushrooms, roasted tomatoes, or chunky vegetables.

MISO: A staple in Asian cuisines, miso is fermented soybean paste. It comes in several varieties that may include another ingredient in addition to the soybeans, such as barley or rice. Pungent and salty, miso is best known as the base for Japanese-style soups, and is also useful for making sauces, dressings, and dips.

PEANUT SATAY SAUCE: This readymade sauce is one of my favorites. It adds a blast of flavor to Thai-style vegetable and noodle dishes and is also an excellent salad dressing.

PESTO: There are more ready-made vegan pesto sauces than ever, most based on basil and nuts like traditional pestos, but ditching the dairy. Look for them in the pasta aisle or produce section of supermarkets and Natural foods stores.

SALSA: Salsa comes in tons of great varieties that give you choices beyond the heat level. Smoky chipotle, cilantro-garlic, and salsa verde are just a few to explore. I call for salsa verde (made with tomatillos) in a few recipes; it has an unusual flavor that adds bold notes to dishes.

SALAD DRESSINGS: Keeping a couple of different salad dressings goes a long way to inspiring more salad-eating! Vinaigrette (basic, balsamic, or raspberry) and vegan French dressing are two useful basics. Much as I enjoy shortcuts, I often make my own dressings. It takes almost no time and is more economical. You'll find a few easy recipes on pages 71 to 73.

SOY SAUCE OR TAMARI: What is labeled as tamari (or in some instances labeled shoyu-tamari) is actually what's known in Japan as shoyu. True tamari is rare in this country, so when you buy a product labeled tamari, chances are very good that you are really buying shoyu, or natural soy sauce. Choose a naturally brewed brand with reduced sodium content.

TERIYAKI MARINADE: Taking soy sauce (one of its ingredients) a step further, this bottled sauce also usually includes rice vinegar, molasses, sugar, onion, garlic, and sesame seeds. Strict vegans should be aware that some brands contain honey, so check labels. Teriyaki marinade gives a full-bodied flavor and what's known as a "lacquered" finish to Asian-style dishes.

VEGAN MAYONNAISE: This is a product I can't live without, so I won't try. My favorite, hands down, is Vegenaise®. It's a staple in natural foods stores, and increasingly, well-stocked supermarkets, often shelved near the tofu products. Use vegan mayonnaise in sandwiches, wraps, slaws, and to make dressings.

NUTS, NUT BUTTERS, AND SEEDS

Unless you have allergies, don't overlook nuts as a fantastic protein source. A sprinkling of nuts boosts the flavor and nutrition of grain and pasta dishes, salads, stir-fries, and desserts.

A few to consider keeping on hand regularly are almonds, cashews, peanuts, and walnuts. Seeds you'll find useful include pumpkin, sunflower, and sesame. Hemp seeds—a fine source of valuable fatty acids—are great as well. Nuts and seeds are perishable, so buy them in small quantities and refrigerate them in the warmer months to prevent rancidity.

As for nut butters, choose natural varieties with no added fats, salt, sugar, and preservatives. Nut butters tend to be expensive, so it's fine to stick with peanut butter if you're on a budget. But do spring the little extra for an organic brand; conventional peanuts tend to be grown with a lot of pesticides.

TOFU, TEMPEH, AND SEITAN

There's a chapter ahead dedicated to what I call "the protein trio." If these will be a regular part of your reportoire, here are the basics:

TOFU: Tofu fans will want to keep a standard 14-ounce tub or two in the fridge. Extra-firm is the preferred choice for most of the recipes in this book. We'll make good use of baked tofu as well. Aseptic packages of firm and extra-firm silken tofu don't need to be refrigerated, so those can be regular or occasional pantry items.

TEMPEH: A fermented soy food, tempeh comes in 8-ounce packages. It's more of an acquired taste than tofu and is considered one of the more digestible forms of soy. Purchase as needed or keep on hand in the refrigerator.

SEITAN: An appealing protein alternative to soy products, seitan's main drawback is that it's pure wheat gluten—so it's not for everyone. The widely marketed White Wave seitan products found in natural foods stores (and increasingly, in supermarkets) are quite good. This is another protein product you can choose to keep on hand or purchase as needed and keep refrigerated.

1

APPETIZERS & SNACKS

I can't say why, but vegan cookbooks seem to offer scant recipes for appetizers. On the other hand, collections (vegan or otherwise) that focus singularly on the subject often present recipes that are overly complicated. Who wants to make an appetizer that takes longer to make than an entire meal? For me, that takes the fun out of it.

While not exhaustive, this chapter presents a sampling of **EASY, WARM, AND COOL APPETIZERS**, including dips and spreads. Mainly based on vegetables and beans, these **GUILT-FREE BITES** make nice first courses or **SNACKS TO ENJOY** on their own.

SCALLION PANCAKES

Scallion pancakes are a classic appetizer on Chinese take-out menus and are usually safe for vegans. The only problem is that they're often as greasy as they are irresistible. Here is a homemade recipe that lets you be in control of the oil content. You can serve these scallion pancakes as part of an Asian-themed dinner, and they're fantastic with many kinds of soups, Asian-inspired or otherwise.

MAKES ABOUT TWO DOZEN 3-INCH PANCAKES

1 cup whole-wheat pastry flour or spelt flour, or a combination

1 cup plus 2 tablespoons water

½ teaspoon salt

1 heaping cup thinly sliced scallions

High-heat vegetable oil (such as safflower)

Sweet chili sauce or teriyaki marinade for serving (or see following recipe for Sweet & Savory Dipping Sauce)

OPTIONAL ADDITION

* Add a tablespoon or two of sesame seeds to the batter.

1. Combine the flour, water, and salt in a mixing bowl. Whisk together to get a smooth batter.

2. Stir in the scallions.

3. Heat a lightly oiled nonstick griddle or wide skillet. When nice and hot, ladle the batter onto the skillet in ¼-cup quantities. If the batter doesn't spread nicely, add a little more water and whisk to combine. Cook the pancakes on both sides until golden brown. Remove each batch to a covered container, lining each layer with paper towels to absorb excess oil.

4. Once all the pancakes are cooked, serve warm with the sauce of your choice.

SWEET & SAVORY DIPPING SAUCE

This is not only perfect to serve with the preceding recipe for Scallion Pancakes, it's also good with vegetable spring rolls or dumplings from the supermarket or the natural foods store's freezer section. Sometimes they come with sauce, but it's often not enough.

MAKES ABOUT ½ CUP

⅓ cup all-fruit apricot or peach preserves

2 tablespoons orange juice or mango nectar

1 tablespoon reduced-sodium soy sauce

1 tablespoon rice vinegar or white wine vinegar

1 to 2 teaspoons grated fresh or jarred ginger

1. Combine all the ingredients in a small bowl and stir together until well blended. Serve as suggested in the headnote.

2. Store any unused portion in an airtight container in the refrigerator.

BAKED POLENTA FRIES

Baked polenta fries have become a food blog trend, but most recipes involve a lengthy process. Polenta (coarse cornmeal) is cooked from scratch, spread into a dish, and cooled for hours to firm up. Only then can it be cut into fry shapes. We're talking at least three hours of prep and wait time before they even go into the oven!

Here we'll cut to the chase with precooked polenta—the kind that comes in those neat tubes. Hours of prep and wait time are reduced to mere minutes. These offbeat fries are a tasty appetizer or snack served on their own; they also make a nice side dish served with veggie burgers, wraps, sandwiches, and main-dish salads.

3 TO 4 SERVINGS

1 (16-ounce) tube polenta

Olive oil or other vegetable oil, as needed

Salt and freshly ground pepper, to taste

Ketchup or marinara sauce for serving

1. Preheat the oven to 425°F. If your oven runs hot or you're baking something else at the same time, 400°F works, too.

2. Cut the polenta in half crosswise, then cut each section lengthwise into fry shapes, about ½-inch thick.

3. Put the polenta fries into a bowl and drizzle in a little oil (not too much, just enough to coat lightly), toss together gently to distribute, and sprinkle with a little salt and pepper.

4. Arrange the fries in a single layer on a parchment-lined baking sheet or in a shallow roasting pan. Bake for 20 to 25 minutes, turning every few minutes, or until crispy and firm on the outside.

5. Serve at once with ketchup or marinara sauce.

OPTIONAL ADDITION

* After drizzling the polenta fries with oil, sprinkle in a little dried oregano or thyme, or an Italian seasoning blend.

BAKED TOFU NUGGETS

As they bake, these neat little tofu nuggets become firm and chewy. Kids love them as a main dish or snack, and as an easy appetizer for adults, they disappear quickly! Consider doubling the recipe for a party-size gathering.

4 TO 6 SERVINGS

1 (14- to 16-ounce) tub extra-firm tofu

1 tablespoon olive oil

3 tablespoons fine cornmeal or garbanzo flour

1½ teaspoons salt-free seasoning blend

¼ teaspoon salt

Freshly ground pepper to taste

Warmed marinara or barbecue sauce, or ketchup for serving

1. Preheat the oven to 425°F.

2. Cut the tofu crosswise into ½-inch-thick slices to get 6 slabs. Blot well between clean tea towels or several layers of paper towels (or use a tofu press ahead of time). Cut each slab crosswise into 4 nuggets, each about ½ by 2 inches.

3. In a large mixing bowl, gently toss the tofu with the oil until evenly coated. Combine the cornmeal, seasoning blend, salt, and freshly ground pepper in a large plastic freezer bag or produce bag and shake to combine. Add the tofu nuggets and shake gently until evenly coated.

4. Arrange the nuggets in a single layer on a lightly oiled nonstick baking sheet. Bake for 15 minutes, then turn them carefully and bake for another 10 minutes, or until golden and firm.

5. Serve at once with the sauce of your choice.

WAYS TO MAKE SKILLET-ROASTED CHICKPEAS

Roasted chickpeas have become a popular snack. And why not? Chickpeas are arguably the tastiest members of the legume family. Pan-roasting chickpeas on the stovetop is ultimately quicker and more efficient than heating up your oven. In addition to simply enjoying them as an appetizer or snack, skillet-roasted chickpeas are a tasty topping for salads and pasta dishes.

SRIRACHA-LEMON CHICKPEAS

Sriracha fans will enjoy these spicy, tart, and slightly sweet skillet-roasted chickpeas. With this recipe and the others that follow, feel free to adjust the flavorings to your taste.

3 TO 4 SERVINGS

1 teaspoon olive oil or vegetable oil

1 teaspoon sriracha

1 tablespoon maple syrup or agave nectar

1 tablespoon lemon juice

1 (15-ounce) can chickpeas, drained and rinsed

1. Combine all the ingredients in a medium skillet, making sure that the chickpeas are evenly coated. Bring the mixture to a simmer and cook for 8 minutes or so over medium-high heat, stirring often, until the chickpeas are nicely glazed.

2. Adjust the sriracha, maple syrup, and lemon juice to taste, then cook the chickpeas, stirring constantly, for 2 to 4 minutes longer, until lightly browned. Remove from the heat and transfer to a serving bowl.

SESAME-GINGER CHICKPEAS

Sesame-ginger salad dressing gives these roasted chickpeas a lovely glaze. Watch them disappear quickly!

3 TO 4 SERVINGS

- 2 tablespoons bottled sesame-ginger salad dressing
- 2 teaspoons maple syrup or agave nectar
- 1 (15-ounce) can chickpeas, drained and rinsed
- ½ teaspoon ground ginger, or more to taste
- 2 teaspoons sesame seeds

1. Shake the bottle of sesame-ginger dressing well before measuring it out. Combine the dressing and agave in a medium skillet with the chickpeas. Cook for 8 minutes or so over medium-high heat, stirring often, until nicely glazed.

2. Add the ginger and taste, adjusting the flavors if you'd like. Cook the chickpeas, stirring constantly, for 2 to 4 minutes longer, until lightly browned. Sprinkle in the sesame seeds. Remove from the heat and transfer to a serving bowl.

CURRY-LIME CHICKPEAS

Chickpeas are always compatible with curry flavors. In addition to enjoying this variation of skillet-roasted chickpeas as a snack, use it as a topping for grain or vegetable dishes.

3 TO 4 SERVINGS

- 1 teaspoon olive oil or vegetable oil
- 1 tablespoon lime juice
- 1 tablespoon vegan mayonnaise
- 1 (15-ounce) can chickpeas, drained and rinsed
- 1 teaspoon curry powder, or more to taste
- Sriracha or other hot sauce to taste

1. Combine the oil, lime juice, vegan mayonnaise, and chickpeas in a medium skillet. Cook for 8 minutes or so over medium-high heat, stirring often, until nicely glazed.

2. Add the curry powder and hot sauce and cook the chickpeas, stirring constantly, for 2 to 4 minutes longer, until lightly browned. Remove from the heat and transfer to a serving bowl.

SMOKY BBQ CHICKPEAS

Barbecue seasonings have become one of my favorite spice blends. Even when used in small amounts, they deliver big flavor. Look for them in the spice section of well-stocked supermarkets.

3 TO 4 SERVINGS

- 1 teaspoon olive oil or vegetable oil
- 2 teaspoons maple syrup or agave nectar
- 2 teaspoons soy sauce or liquid aminos
- 1 (15-ounce) can chickpeas, drained and rinsed
- 1 teaspoon barbecue seasoning (try mesquite or smoky maple)

1. Combine all the ingredients except the barbecue seasoning in a medium skillet, making sure that the chickpeas are coated. Cook for 8 minutes or so over medium-high heat, stirring often, until nicely glazed.

2. Add the barbecue seasoning and cook the chickpeas, stirring constantly, for 2 to 4 minutes longer, until lightly browned. Remove from the heat and transfer to a serving bowl.

MAPLE-CINNAMON CHICKPEAS

Sweet chickpeas? Somehow, this really works. Along with the maple syrup, a coating of cinnamon and a tiny bit of sugar make these go down like candy.

3 TO 4 SERVINGS

- 1 teaspoon neutral vegetable oil
- 2 tablespoons maple syrup
- 1 (15-ounce) can chickpeas, drained and rinsed
- ½ teaspoon cinnamon
- ½ teaspoon natural granulated sugar

1. Combine the oil and syrup in a medium skillet with the chickpeas. Cook for 8 minutes or so over medium-high heat, stirring often, until the chickpeas are nicely glazed.

2. Sprinkle in the cinnamon and sugar, then cook the chickpeas, stirring constantly, for 2 to 4 minutes longer, until lightly browned. Remove from the heat and transfer to a serving bowl.

BRUSCHETTA

The dips and spreads that follow (pages 11 to 19) are fantastic on bruschetta, which is basically fresh baguette or Italian bread, sliced and oven-toasted until crisp. Use whole-grain bread for added goodness.

8 OR MORE SERVINGS

1 long fresh baguette or Italian bread (not too skinny)

Olive oil cooking spray or extra-virgin olive oil

1 large clove garlic, halved

Spread of your choice for serving

1. Preheat the oven to 350°F.

2. Cut the bread into ½-inch-thick slices. Arrange the bread slices in a single layer on a parchment-lined baking sheet and spray the tops lightly with cooking spray or brush lightly with olive oil.

3. Bake the bread for 7 minutes, then turn the pieces over, spray or brush lightly again, and continue to bake for 5 to 7 minutes longer, or until golden and crisp. Remove from the oven and cool completely.

4. When cool enough to handle, rub one side of each toast with the cut side of the garlic.

5. Serve in a napkin-lined bowl or basket with a spread of choice.

OLIVE AND DRIED TOMATO TAPENADE

If olive tapenade and dried tomato tapenade are both crazy-good, it stands to reason that the two combined would be a dream team. Tapenade is a perfect go-to appetizer for last-minute guests. Serve with whole-grain crackers, sliced fresh Italian or French bread, or Bruschetta (page 10).

8 OR MORE SERVINGS

¾ cup pitted brine-cured black olives such as Kalamata

½ cup sun-dried tomatoes (see Note)

½ cup fresh parsley leaves, plus more for garnish

¼ cup walnut or pecan pieces

1 tablespoon fresh or bottled lemon juice, or to taste

Freshly ground pepper to taste

1. Combine all the ingredients in a food processor with ¼ cup water. Pulse on and off until everything is finely and evenly chopped. If need be, add a little more water to help the mixture come together.

2. Transfer the tapenade to a small serving bowl and serve as suggested in the headnote.

3. Store any unused portion in an airtight container in the refrigerator, where it will keep for at least a week.

NOTE
The sun-dried tomatoes for this recipe must be nice and moist. If you're using dried tomatoes that aren't oil-cured, soak them in hot water for a few minutes before using if need be.

GREEN PEA AND CASHEW SPREAD OR DIP

This lively green spread or dip is fantastic on fresh bread, Bruschetta (page 10), or whole-grain crackers, but my favorite way to serve it is with brightly colored vegetables—sliced bell peppers, yellow squash, carrots, and even raw sweet potato.

MAKES ABOUT 1½ CUPS

1 tablespoon olive oil

1 medium onion, chopped

1 cup frozen green peas, completely thawed

⅔ cup toasted cashews

¼ cup fresh parsley leaves or a few sprigs fresh dill

Juice of ½ lemon or lime, plus more, to taste

Salt and freshly ground pepper, to taste

1. Heat the oil in a medium skillet. Add the onion and sauté until lightly browned, stirring occasionally.

2. In a food processor, combine the onion and all remaining ingredients except the salt and pepper with ¼ cup water. Pulse the mixture until it is an even, coarse puree, stopping occasionally to scrape down the sides of the bowl.

3. Taste the spread and add a little more lemon juice if you'd like, then season with salt and pepper. Pulse the processor on and off a few times, then transfer to a serving bowl. Serve as suggested in the headnote.

4. Store any unused portion in an airtight container in the refrigerator, where it will keep for 3 or 4 days.

CREAMY ARTICHOKE DIP

If you enjoy artichokes, you'll love this tangy dip that takes no more than 5 minutes to make. Look for vegan sour cream in natural foods stores. Serve with veggie chips, tortilla chips, or raw vegetables. It's also great on Bruschetta (page 10).

MAKES ABOUT 1½ CUPS

1 (6-to 8-ounce) jar marinated artichoke hearts

1 cup vegan sour cream

1 tablespoon lemon or lime juice (fresh or bottled)

1 tablespoon chopped fresh dill (or ½ teaspoon dried)

1 scallion, green part only, thinly sliced, or a few finely chopped fresh chives

Salt and freshly ground pepper, to taste

1. Drain the artichoke hearts. Remove and discard any tough outer leaves, then chop the artichoke hearts coarsely.

2. In a small serving bowl, combine the artichoke hearts with the remaining ingredients and stir together. Serve as suggested above in the headnote.

3. Store any unused portion in an airtight container in the refrigerator, where it will keep for 3 or 4 days.

ROASTED RED PEPPER DIP

The intense flavor of roasted red peppers gives this dip a smoky-savory flavor that you can push in one flavor direction or another depending on whether you use smoked or sweet paprika. Serve with a platter of colorful raw vegetables or with whole-grain crackers, fresh bread, or Bruschetta (page 10).

MAKES ABOUT 1½ CUPS

¾ cup firm silken tofu (about half of a 12.3-ounce package)

6 to 8 ounces roasted red peppers (from the supermarket olive bar or a jar), drained

A handful of cilantro or parsley leaves

2 tablespoons lemon or lime juice, or to taste

1 teaspoon smoked or sweet paprika, or more, to taste

Salt and freshly ground pepper, to taste

1. Combine all the ingredients in a food processor. Process the mixture until smooth.

2. Transfer the dip to a serving bowl and serve as suggested in the headnote.

3. Store any unused portion in an airtight container in the refrigerator, where it will keep for 3 or 4 days.

HOMEMADE HUMMUS

Everyone loves hummus—or at least, everyone I know! Starting in the early 2000s, it became one of the fastest-growing items in the snack food category and has stayed that way ever since. While ready-made hummus is available almost everywhere food is sold, I still enjoy making my own. Somehow, no matter what the variety, the store-bought kind tastes the same to me. And this DIY version is more economical, yielding a larger quantity.

Hummus is useful as a spread for fresh pita as an appetizer, as well as in sandwiches and wraps. It's also nice as a dip for a variety of cut fresh vegetables—carrots, bell peppers, turnips, and celery.

6 TO 8 SERVINGS

1 (15-ounce) can chickpeas, drained and rinsed

¼ cup tahini (sesame paste)

1 to 2 cloves garlic, crushed (see Note)

Juice of 1 lemon

Pinch of salt

Freshly ground pepper, to taste

1. Combine all the ingredients in a food processor with ¼ cup water. Process the mixture until smoothly pureed. Add any one of the optional additions listed below as directed.

2. Transfer the hummus to a serving bowl and add an optional garnish, if desired. Serve as suggested in the headnote.

3. Store any unused portion in an airtight container in the refrigerator, where it will keep for up to 4 days.

NOTE
For some aficionados, hummus isn't the same without garlic, but since I'm not a fan of raw garlic, I sauté it first in a tiny bit of olive oil until golden. Truth be told, if I'm going to be incorporating any of the ingredients on page 18, I sometimes skip the garlic altogether.

OPTIONAL ADDITIONS

Prepare any one of the following as directed and add to the food processor once the hummus is already smooth. Pulse until the additional ingredient is finely chopped, not pureed:

* **ROASTED RED PEPPER:** Use 1 to 2 whole roasted peppers. Chop coarsely before adding to the food processor.

* **SUN-DRIED TOMATO:** Use about ½ cup moist sun-dried tomatoes.

* **SPINACH:** Wilt a couple of big handfuls of baby spinach, or use raw.

* **MUSHROOMS:** My favorite! Wilt a cup or so of sliced brown mushrooms in a skillet and drain before adding to the food processor.

* **HERB:** Use about ½ cup fresh parsley or cilantro leaves, or ¼ cup fresh dill.

* **FRESH CHILE:** Use 1 to 2 jalapeños or other fresh hot chile peppers, seeded and chopped.

* **WHOLE CHICKPEAS AND OLIVE OIL:** Garnish the top of the hummus with some whole chickpeas, a drizzle of olive oil, and some paprika.

SPINACH, AVOCADO & TAHINI DIP

This flavor- and nutrition-packed dip, adapted from my book *Wild About Greens*, is one of the recipes I like to use in food demonstrations. It's always practically inhaled. In fact, one audience begged me to make another batch after demolishing the first! Since it's so quick to make, I obliged. Richly flavored, this dip is fantastic with tortilla chips, fresh pita or pita chips, raw vegetables, or a combination.

You can use either lightly steamed or uncooked spinach; the difference will be more of texture than flavor. Lightly steaming the spinach results in a little smoother texture. But if you're a raw foods fan (or just want to skip a step), leaving the spinach uncooked is fine.

MAKES ABOUT 1½ CUPS

4 to 5 ounces baby spinach, rinsed

1 large ripe avocado, peeled and diced

⅓ cup tahini (sesame paste)

Juice of 1 lemon

Chopped fresh parsley, cilantro, or dill

Salt and freshly ground pepper, to taste

1. If you'd like to lightly steam the spinach for a smoother texture, place it in a large skillet or saucepan, and cook over medium heat until just wilted down. Remove from the heat and drain off the excess liquid. Otherwise, just use the raw spinach.

2. Place the cooked (or raw) spinach and all remaining ingredients in a food processor and process until smooth. (If you're using uncooked spinach, add it in batches.) Drizzle in ¼ cup water, or as needed, to keep the mixture moving.

3. Transfer the dip to a serving bowl. Serve at once as suggested in the headnote.

4. Store any unused portion in an airtight container in the refrigerator, where it will keep for up to 2 days.

QUICK REFRIGERATOR PICKLES

Here's a quick way to make refrigerator pickles that I hope you'll love as much as I do. There's no need for traditional canning methods and equipment other than a quart jar. I like to have these in the fridge as often as possible for a crunchy, nearly calorie-free snack. They're also a classic accompaniment to serve with veggie burgers, sandwiches, and wraps.

I recommend using organic or hothouse cucumbers since conventional cukes are a high-pesticide vegetable. And, of course, they should be unwaxed. Don't limit yourself to cucumbers—this works with other vegetables, as suggested (see Variations).

MAKES 1 QUART

2 medium cucumbers, 1 long hothouse cucumber, or 5 to 6 Kirby cucumbers

1 tablespoon salt

2 tablespoons natural granulated sugar

1 to 2 cloves garlic, minced

1 teaspoon dill seed, ½ teaspoon dried dill, or several sprigs fresh dill

¼ cup apple cider vinegar (preferably organic raw ACV, such as Bragg)

1. No matter what kind of cucumber you're using, cut them into 4- to 5-inch spears.

2. Combine the salt and sugar in a cup of hot water and stir until dissolved. Pour into a quart jar, then stir in the garlic, dill, and vinegar.

3. Pack the cucumbers spears upright in the jar, then fill the jar almost to the top with water, covering the cucumbers completely.

4. Cover the jar tightly and store the pickles in the refrigerator. They're usually ready in 24 hours, but if you can wait 48 hours, they'll be that much better!

TIPS

You can use the same liquid for your next batch of pickles after the first batch has been eaten, though they'll be a bit milder in flavor than the first batch.

When you make your next fresh batch of pickles, tailor the flavors to your liking—add more or less salt, sugar, garlic, and/or vinegar.

OPTIONAL ADDITIONS

If you'd like, add either or both of these to the brine:

- ✳ 1 teaspoon whole peppercorns
- ✳ 2 teaspoons pickling spice

VARIATIONS

The following vegetables all can be pickled using this recipe:

- ✳ Asparagus spears (blanched)
- ✳ Beets (cooked and sliced)
- ✳ Bok choy stems
- ✳ Chard stems
- ✳ Carrot slices or spears (or whole baby carrots)
- ✳ Cauliflower (cut into small florets)
- ✳ Mushrooms (medium caps—cleaned, stemmed, and lightly steamed or used raw)
- ✳ Radishes (halved or quartered)
- ✳ Zucchini (thinly sliced or cut into spears)

SUPER-EASY GUACAMOLE

Five minutes, five ingredients, and you've got nearly-instant, really yummy guacamole. Just open a bag of stone-ground tortilla chips, and have a party!

MAKES ABOUT 1½ CUPS

1 medium ripe (mashable but not mushy) avocado, pitted and peeled

¾ cup prepared salsa of your choice (see Note)

1 to 2 tablespoons lime or lemon juice, to taste

¼ to ½ cup chopped fresh cilantro

½ teaspoon ground cumin

1. Cut the avocado into chunks. Place the chunks in a bowl and mash well with a fork. Add the remaining ingredients and stir together well.

2. Serve at once with tortilla chips.

3. Store any unused portion in an airtight container in the refrigerator, where it will keep for a day or two.

NOTE
The heat level of this guacamole depends on the kind of salsa you choose, from mild to incendiary. Try salsa verde, a terrific choice to use in this preparation.

TOFU "FETA"

Serve this with an assortment of olives and/or other brined veggies from your supermarket's olive bar as a simple appetizer. These faux-feta chunks are also delectable as a salad topping.

3 TO 4 SERVINGS

8 ounces extra-firm tofu

3 tablespoons lemon juice

2 tablespoons extra-virgin olive oil

¼ teaspoon salt

¼ teaspoon oregano

1. Slice the tofu into 4 slabs, crosswise. Blot between layers of paper towels, or clean tea towels until you get out as much moisture as you can. Cut the slabs into ½-inch dice.

2. Place in a flat container in a single layer. Toss with the lemon juice and oil; sprinkle with the salt and oregano. Let stand for 30 minutes, then serve as suggested in the headnote.

2

SOUPS

'd venture to say that soups are the **MOST CHALLENGING KIND OF DISH** to make with just five ingredients. And that's coming from someone who's not only a major soup fan, but who has written an entire book on the subject.

To achieve full-bodied flavor, soups benefit from a melding of **WELL-CHOSEN INGREDIENTS AND SEASONINGS**. The recipes that follow, perhaps even more than others in this book, rely on a **SPECIAL TWIST OR FLAVOR-BOOSTING** ingredient. When you crave a good bowl of soup ASAP, the selections in this chapter are yours to enjoy in thirty minutes or less—from prep to table. Soups are perfect partners with salads, wraps, and sandwiches, and of course, simply served with fresh bread.

BUTTERNUT SQUASH SOUP WITH SPINACH & PEAS

Soups based on pureed butternut squash are bowls of pure comfort. While prepping a whole fresh butternut squash is a worthy project when you've got the time and inclination, it's not a route to a quick soup. This one starts with butternut squash puree that comes in 32-ounce containers; Imagine® and Pacific Foods™ brands are equally good.

4 SERVINGS

1 (32-ounce) container butternut squash soup

2 cups frozen green peas, thawed

2 scallions, thinly sliced

2 teaspoons curry powder or garam masala, or to taste

4 to 5 ounces baby spinach

Salt and freshly ground pepper, to taste

1. Pour the contents of the carton of butternut squash soup into a soup pot along with the peas, scallions, and curry powder.

2. Bring the mixture to a rapid simmer and cook for just a couple of minutes, until the peas are heated through and the soup is piping hot.

3. Add the spinach to the soup pot (in batches if need be), then cover and cook until just wilted. Season with salt and pepper and serve at once.

OPTIONAL ADDITIONS

* To make this a main-dish soup, add a 28-ounce can of chickpeas (drained and rinsed).

* Spice it up with sriracha or other hot sauce to taste.

* Garnish the soup with chopped fresh cilantro.

COMPLETE THE MEAL

Serve with fresh bread or flatbread and any kind of mixed-greens salad. Consider Mixed Greens with Apple or Pear, Avocado & Walnuts (page 47).

An easy wrap is also a great partner for this soup. Spread a large soft wrap with Homemade Hummus (see page 17 if you want to make your own); arrange sliced tomatoes, avocado, and lettuce or tender greens down the center. Roll up and repeat as needed.

RED LENTIL SOUP WITH LEAFY GREENS

Tiny red lentils cook quickly, making them a superb base for a protein-packed soup. Embellished with tender greens, this substantial soup can be on the table in less than 30 minutes. Its flavor secret is delicious Indian simmer sauce.

6 SERVINGS

1½ tablespoons olive oil

2 medium onions, chopped

4 cloves garlic, minced

2 cups red lentils, rinsed

1 (12- to 15-ounce) jar Indian simmer sauce of your choice (see Notes)

4 to 6 ounces tender leafy greens, rinsed (see Notes)

Salt and freshly ground pepper, to taste

1. Heat the oil in a soup pot. Add the onions and sauté over medium heat until translucent. Add the garlic and continue to sauté until both vegetables are golden.

2. Add 5 cups of water to the pot, followed by the lentils. Bring the mixture to a slow boil, then lower the heat, cover, and simmer gently until the lentils are mushy, 15 to 20 minutes.

3. Stir in the Indian simmer sauce and greens and cook for 5 to 10 minutes longer, just until the greens are wilted and the soup is piping hot.

4. If the soup is too thick, adjust the consistency with more water. Season with salt and pepper and serve at once.

OPTIONAL ADDITIONS

∗ Crumble pita crisps on top of the soup if you're not serving the soup with fresh pita or other bread.

∗ Replace 2 cups of the water with a 15-ounce can of coconut milk for a richer flavor.

∗ Garnish the soup with chopped fresh cilantro.

NOTES

Make this soup as spicy or mild as you'd like with your choice of simmer sauce. See more on **Indian simmer sauces** on page xv.

For utmost convenience, use baby spinach, baby arugula, baby kale, or baby "power greens," none of which need to be prepped at all. If you have more time, patience, and a batch of other greens in the fridge, by all means, use them! Kale, collards, or chard work well in this soup. Stem and chop them into bite-size pieces and rinse well. They might need to cook just a bit longer than the baby varieties of greens.

COMPLETE THE MEAL

This main-dish soup needs only fresh bread or pita and any kind of green salad to complete it. If you need bit of inspiration, see **Mixed Greens with Apple or Pear, Avocado & Walnuts** (page 47).

INDIAN-SPICED CAULIFLOWER & RED BEAN SOUP

Here's a hearty soup that, like the previous recipe, relies on Indian simmer sauce for a bold flavor. Containing deliciously complex blends of seasonings typical to Indian cuisine, Indian simmer sauces are ideal soup starters.

6 SERVINGS

4 to 5 heaping cups cauliflower florets, cut into small florets

2 (15-ounce) cans kidney or red beans, drained and rinsed

1 (12-to 15-ounce) jar Indian simmer sauce of your choice (see Note)

1 (15-ounce) can light coconut milk

½ cup chopped fresh cilantro

Salt and freshly ground pepper, to taste

1. Combine the cauliflower with 2 cups water in a soup pot. Bring to a slow boil, then lower the heat and simmer, covered, for 8 to 10 minutes, or just until tender.

2. Add the red beans, Indian simmer sauce, and coconut milk. Bring to a rapid simmer, then lower the heat, cover, and continue to cook just until everything is piping hot, not more than 5 minutes. If the soup is too thick, stir in a little water as needed.

3. Stir in the cilantro, then season with salt and pepper. Serve at once.

NOTE

Make this soup as spicy or mild as you'd like with your choice of simmer sauce. See more on Indian simmer sauces on page xv.

OPTIONAL ADDITION

* Add 2 to 3 sliced scallions to the soup when adding the cilantro.

LESS TIME / EVEN LAZIER

Use a 16-ounce bag of chopped cauliflower florets instead of fresh.

COMPLETE THE MEAL

Like the previous recipe, this main-dish soup needs only fresh bread or pita and any kind of green salad to complete it. Or, if you want to skip the bread, serve with Almond Basmati Rice Pilaf (page 134).

COCONUT-SWEET POTATO BISQUE

For this cheerful, orange-hued soup, microwaving rather than peeling and dicing several big sweet potatoes cuts way down on prep time. But if you're not a fan of microwaving, peel and dice to your heart's content! That option is given in the note following the recipe.

6 SERVINGS

4 large or 5 medium-large sweet potatoes (see More Time / Less Lazy)

1 tablespoon olive oil

1 large onion, chopped

1 (15-ounce) can fire-roasted diced tomatoes

1 (15-ounce) can light coconut milk

2 teaspoons good-quality curry powder

Salt and freshly ground pepper, to taste

1. Microwave the sweet potatoes, starting with 3 minutes per potato. Test, then add an additional minute per potato until soft. Set aside until cool enough to handle. If you want to speed up the process, immerse them in a bowl of ice water.

2. When the sweet potatoes are cool enough to handle, split them in half, scoop the flesh out into a bowl, and discard the skins.

3. Heat the oil in a soup pot. Add the onion and sauté until golden. Add the tomatoes, coconut milk, curry powder, and 2 cups water. Bring to a slow boil. Stir in the sweet potato flesh.

4. Puree the soup until smooth either by using an immersion blender or a blender (in batches, if necessary).

5. Heat the soup gently until it reaches a simmer, then season with salt and pepper. Serve at once, or, if time allows, let it stand for a half hour or longer to allow the flavors to blend. Heat through gently as needed.

OPTIONAL ADDITIONS
* Add some heat with sriracha or other hot sauce.
* Garnish the top of each serving with chopped cilantro.

MORE TIME / LESS LAZY
Instead of microwaving the sweet potatoes, peel and cut them into large dice. Place in a large saucepan with barely enough water to cover. Bring to a slow boil, then lower the heat, cover, and simmer until tender, 15 to 20 minutes. Proceed with the recipe. If there's still some cooking water remaining in the pan with the sweet potatoes, use less water before adding the sweet potatoes to the tomato mixture, then adjust as needed.

COMPLETE THE MEAL
Serve the bisque with something sandwich-y. I suggest either **Tofu, Arugula & Olive Wraps** (page 177) or **"Tofuna" Sandwich Spread** (page 171) on fresh bread.

NEARLY-INSTANT MISO SOUP

If you're vegan and love the miso soup served in Japanese eateries, I have bad news for you. It's often made with fish ingredients like bonito, so make sure to ask when ordering! It's nice to know that producing a reasonable facsimile at home (minus the fish) is a snap to make. In my version, dark green lettuce leaves stand in for kombu, a standard ingredient of miso soup. I'm not crazy about the fishy flavor and slippery texture of sea vegetables, so the leafy greens suit my taste. I hope they'll do the same for you.

4 TO 6 SERVINGS

1 (32-ounce) container low-sodium vegetable broth

1 (12.3-ounce) container extra-firm silken tofu

2 to 4 tablespoons miso, to taste

2 to 3 scallions, green parts only, thinly sliced

About ½ head romaine or other dark green lettuce, chopped

Freshly ground pepper, to taste

1. Bring the broth to a slow boil in a small soup pot.

2. Stir in the tofu and cook until the broth returns to a rapid simmer, then turn the heat down to low.

3. Dissolve the desired amount of miso in just enough warm water to make it pourable before stirring it into the broth. The more miso you use, the more pungent and salty the soup will be, so start with less, and add more until the soup is salty/pungent to your liking. Stir in the scallions and lettuce. Season with pepper and serve at once.

OPTIONAL ADDITION

✳ Add a teaspoon or two of grated fresh or jarred ginger.

COMPLETE THE MEAL

Serve the soup as a first course followed by Hoisin-Ginger Udon Noodles (page 111) or pick up a few rolls of store-bought sushi to serve with the soup. Either way, a platter of baby carrots and sliced turnips or radishes is welcome.

MISO SOUP WITH MUSHROOMS, BOK CHOY & TOFU

Here's another basic miso soup featuring two ingredients meant for each other—mushrooms and bok choy.

4 TO 6 SERVINGS

1½ to 2 cups cremini and/or shiitake mushrooms, cleaned, stemmed, and sliced

8 ounces firm tofu, well-drained and cut into small dice

2 to 3 scallions, green parts only, thinly sliced

6 to 8 stalks regular bok choy with leaves or 2 baby bok choy

2 to 4 tablespoons miso

Freshly ground pepper, to taste

1. Combine the mushrooms and 5 cups water in a large saucepan and bring to a simmer. Cover and simmer gently for about 10 minutes.

2. Stir in the tofu, scallions, and bok choy. Simmer until the bok choy is barely tender-crisp, about 3 minutes.

3. Dissolve the desired amount of miso in just enough warm water to make it pourable before stirring it into the broth. The more miso you use, the more pungent and salty the soup will be, so start with less, and continue to add it until the soup is salty/pungent to your liking.

4. Season with pepper and serve.

OPTIONAL ADDITIONS

✳ Use snow peas or broccoli instead of, or in addition to, the bok choy.

✳ Add a teaspoon or two of grated fresh or jarred ginger when you stir in the tofu and vegetables.

✳ Add a can of cut baby corn and its liquid when you stir in the tofu and the vegetables.

COMPLETE THE MEAL

For a light meal, serve the soup with Scallion Pancakes (page 2). Or, serve as a first course with Streamlined Vegetable Lo Mein (page 112) or Cold Shirataki Noodles with Lettuce & Sweet Chili Sauce (page 64). For any of these options, a platter of raw vegetables rounds out the meal.

UDON NOODLE SOUP

Asian noodles used to be exclusive to specialty groceries, but now they're a staple in the international food aisles of well-stocked supermarkets. Thick, hearty udon noodles are just one of the varieties you'll find. I prefer the arugula or watercress option in this gingery soup, but spinach works just as well if that's handier.

4 SERVINGS

1 (8-ounce) package udon noodles

1 (32-ounce) container low-sodium vegetable broth

2 to 3 teaspoons grated fresh or jarred ginger, to taste

3 to 4 scallions, thinly sliced

3 to 4 ounces baby arugula, watercress, or baby spinach

Salt and freshly ground pepper to taste

1. Cook the noodles according to the package directions until al dente. Drain in a colander, then use kitchen shears to cut them here and there to shorten.

2. Use the same cooking pot to heat up the broth. When it comes to a simmer, stir in the ginger and scallions. Stir in the cooked noodles and the greens and cook for just a minute or two longer until everything is piping hot.

3. Season with salt and pepper. Add a little water if the ingredients need more breathing room. Serve at once.

VARIATION

＊ Use any other variety of Asian noodles if you prefer. This soup is good with soba (buckwheat noodles) and rice vermicelli as well.

COMPLETE THE MEAL
Serve the soup as a first course with **Lazy General Tso's Tofu** (page 85) or **Seitan Peppersteak** (page 88). Add a platter of baby carrots and cherry or grape tomatoes.

SALSA BLACK BEAN SOUP

This soup hits the spot when you crave something filling and hearty on a chilly, drizzly day or when you feel a cold coming on. Truth be told, I make it any time I want to warm up in a hurry since it only takes about 20 minutes to prepare.

I highly recommend using organic canned black beans because they're packed in a liquid that's like a tasty broth—it's much better than the brine used in conventional brands. Another bonus is that organic beans often come in BPA-free cans. This soup also gets a huge flavor boost from a jar of full-bodied salsa. Thanks to Hannah Brown for this tasty recipe.

4 SERVINGS

1 tablespoon olive oil

1 medium onion, chopped

1 bell pepper, any color, diced

2 teaspoons ground cumin

2 (28-ounce) cans organic black beans, undrained

1 (16-ounce) jar salsa (see Note)

Salt and freshly ground pepper, to taste

1. Heat the oil in a soup pot. Add the onion and sauté over medium heat until translucent, about 3 to 4 minutes. Add the bell pepper and sauté until the onion is golden. Stir in the cumin and sauté for a minute or two longer.

2. Add the beans and salsa. Bring to a slow boil, then lower the heat, cover, and simmer for 6 to 8 minutes longer.

3. Adjust the consistency with a little water if needed, but let the soup stay nice and thick. Taste for salt and pepper, but you might not need much, or any, of either. Serve at once.

VARIATION

* Puree the soup in a blender, in batches if necessary, or by inserting an immersion blender into the soup pot.

NOTE

Choose a robust variety of salsa, like cilantro-garlic. If you like heat, consider chipotle salsa.

OPTIONAL ADDITIONS

The soup is delicious as is, but if you'd like to dress it up, use any one or two of the following toppings:

* Sautéed and crumbled tempeh bacon
* Crumbled tortilla chips
* Wilted spinach or other leafy greens
* Sriracha or other hot sauce

COMPLETE THE MEAL

Perfect partners for this soup are either of the Quesadillas on pages 184 and 186. Any of the Avocado Toast (page 180) options (other than the sweet one) team well with this soup, too.

CREAMY MUSHROOM SOUP

This comforting soup is one of my all-time favorites. You can choose between cannellini beans or silken tofu to create a creamy base for a soup sure to please mushroom fans. Leftovers make a great pasta sauce or topping for grains.

6 SERVINGS

1 tablespoon olive oil)

1 large onion, chopped

2 cloves garlic, minced

1 (15-ounce) can cannellini beans, drained and rinsed, or 12.3-ounce container firm silken tofu

2 cups low-sodium vegetable broth, plus more as needed

10 to 12 ounces cremini or white mushrooms, sliced

(Salt and freshly ground pepper, to taste)

1. Heat the oil in a soup pot. Add the onion and sauté over medium heat until translucent. Add the garlic and continue to sauté until the onion is golden.

2. Transfer the onion and garlic mixture to a food processor along with the cannellini beans or tofu and a little of the broth. Process until smoothly pureed.

3. In the same soup pot, combine the mushrooms with enough water to keep the bottom of the pot moist. Cover and cook until tender, about 8 minutes.

4. Transfer the bean mixture from the food processor to the mushrooms in the soup pot. Add the remaining vegetable broth and stir to combine. If the soup is too thick, add a little more broth.

5. Heat the soup slowly until nicely heated through, but don't let it boil. Season with salt and pepper, and serve. Or, if time allows, let the soup stand off the heat for an hour or so to develop flavor, then heat through as needed.

OPTIONAL ADDITIONS

* Garnish each serving of soup with chopped parsley.

* Top each serving of soup with crisp croutons.

COMPLETE THE MEAL

Serve the soup as a first course followed by an easy grain dish, like **Quinoa with Tender Greens & Artichoke Hearts** (page 129) and one of the **Slaws** on pages 52 to 57. Or, serve with any of the **Avocado Toast** options (page 180), other than the sweet one or the mushroom-topped version, to avoid culinary redundancy!

CREAM OF ASPARAGUS SOUP

Here's an asparagus puree with an appealing green hue (assisted by peas). Now that asparagus has become more of a year-round vegetable, you can enjoy this soup nearly any time of year, but I still recommend making it in the spring, when asparagus is the most flavorful and least expensive.

6 SERVINGS

1 pound asparagus

1 tablespoon olive oil, optional

1 large onion, chopped

2 cups vegetable broth or 2 cups water with 2 vegetable bouillon cubes

8 ounces frozen green peas, thawed

¼ cup chopped fresh dill, plus more for garnish

Salt and freshly ground pepper, to taste

1. Cut about an inch off the bottoms of the asparagus stalks and discard. Scrape any tough skin with a vegetable peeler. Cut the stalks into approximately 1-inch pieces. Set aside the tips.

2. Heat the oil in a large soup pot. Add the onion and sauté until golden. Add the asparagus (minus the tips) and vegetable broth. Bring to a slow boil, then cover, lower the heat, and simmer gently until the asparagus is tender-crisp.

3. Stir in the peas and dill and continue to simmer briefly, until the peas are just tender. (This shouldn't take more than a minute or two—you want them to stay bright green.)

4. Insert an immersion blender into the soup pot and process until smoothly pureed. (Or, with a slotted spoon, transfer the solid ingredients to the container of a food processor or blender. Process until smooth, then transfer back into the liquid in the soup pot and stir until combined.)

5. Add additional broth or water if the soup is too thick. Season with salt and pepper. Serve at once, or let stand for an hour or so to develop flavor, then heat through as needed.

6. Just before serving, steam the reserved asparagus tips until bright green and tender-crisp and use to garnish each serving of soup. Garnish each serving with a few fronds of dill as well.

COMPLETE THE MEAL
Serve the soup with a crusty sourdough bread and **Two-Bean Salad** (page 66). This is also delightful served with **Portobello & Coleslaw Wraps** (page 182) or **"Tofuna" Sandwich Spread** (page 171) on fresh bread.

HOT OR COLD FRESH TOMATO SOUP

This soup is a gift to gardeners with a bumper crop of summer tomatoes. Non-gardeners can make this soup with summer tomatoes from the local farmers' market, of course.

6 SERVINGS

2½ to 3 pounds ripe, flavorful tomatoes, quartered

1 cup spicy tomato juice or vegetable blend juice, or as needed

¼ cup chopped fresh basil, parsley, or dill

1 to 2 scallions, green parts only, thinly sliced

Juice of ½ lemon, or to taste

Salt and freshly ground pepper, to taste

1. Working in batches, process the tomatoes to a coarse puree in a food processor or blender. If you plan on serving this soup hot, transfer each batch to a soup pot. To serve cold, transfer each batch to a serving container.

2. Either way, add the remaining ingredients. To serve hot, heat the soup gently until it comes to a rapid simmer. To serve cold, cover and refrigerate until chilled.

COMPLETE THE MEAL
Served hot, this soup goes beautifully with any of the Grilled Cheese variations on pages 172 to 173. Served cold, try this soup with Baked Tofu & Peanut Satay Wraps (page 178).

5-MINUTE GAZPACHO

Making gazpacho at the height of summer has long been an annual ritual for me, especially when we grow tomatoes. This classic Spanish cold soup isn't that complicated to make, but there's a lot of chopping involved. If you're a fan of gazpacho, but not of chopping, this shortcut version is for you. The brilliant twist to this recipe is fresh salsa—not the kind that comes in jars, but the type sold in the refrigerated section of supermarket produce departments, containing tomatoes, garlic, chile peppers, and herbs. Some brands also contain cucumber and bell pepper—all in teeny, tiny pieces. When summer company is coming and you need a nice first course fast, this quick gazpacho is ideal!

4 TO 6 SERVINGS

1 (16-ounce) container fresh (not jarred) salsa

3 to 4 cups bottled spicy tomato juice, preferably chilled

2 limes

½ cup chopped fresh parsley or cilantro, or to taste

Salt and freshly ground pepper, to taste

1. Combine the salsa and 3 cups of the tomato juice in a serving container.

2. Add the juice of one of the limes. Cut the other lime into wedges for garnish.

3. Stir in as much chopped fresh parsley or cilantro as you'd like.

4. Taste before adding salt and pepper, but you might not need much, or any, of either. Serve at once or chill for a few hours in the refrigerator to develop flavor.

COMPLETE THE MEAL
Keep it super-simple with store-bought veggie burgers on whole-grain buns, or go one tiny step further with **Crazy-Easy Sloppy Joes** (page 175). Another tasty pairing is **Pesto or Hummus Flatbreads** (page 170).

3

SALADS

've always been partial to salads because there's no need to be precise and there's plenty of room for creativity. **TAKE SOME VEGETABLES** (and/or fruit). **TOSS** in a bowl. **ADD DRESSING**. Boom, **YOU'RE DONE**. Whether you like to improvise with eclectic ingredients or stick with tried-and-true harmonies, salad is no longer just about lettuce and tomatoes. With grains, beans, almost any vegetable (raw or even lightly cooked), and even fruit as part of the mix, **THE POSSIBILITIES ARE ENDLESS.**

Salads are an easy way to add nutrition to the plate, along with color, crunch, and flavor. Most of us—vegan, vegetarian, or otherwise—should be eating more fresh raw vegetables. I hope **THIS CHAPTER WILL INSPIRE YOU** to do just that.

WAYS TO MAKE MIXED GREENS SALADS

Baby greens are now a staple in supermarket produce sections, but I remember when they were exclusive to upscale restaurants. They've graduated from fancy terms like "mesclun" to the more democratic-sounding "mixed greens" or "spring mix." No matter what you call them, this blend of tender lettuces is a lovely canvas for other ingredients you toss in with them. Depending on the mix, you might find frisée, radicchio, arugula, mâche, mizuna, and tatsoi among the more common young lettuces. Feel free to use any of these greens. And, in general, feel free to tinker with the following recipes by substituting other ingredients you may have on hand.

You'll notice that the number of servings aren't included in these salad recipes, since you can use whatever quantity of the mixed greens or other ingredients as you'd like. No need for precision here. This is salad, after all!

MIXED GREENS WITH TOMATO, CORN & AVOCADO

Featuring corn kernels, avocado, and tomato, this is a good way to round out Southwestern-style tortilla specialties as well as grain and bean dishes.

Mixed greens, as desired

1 medium firm, ripe avocado

1 or 2 medium tomatoes, diced, or ½ pint cherry or grape tomatoes

1 cup or so lightly cooked fresh or frozen corn kernels

Bottled balsamic or cilantro-lime vinaigrette

1. Combine all the ingredients in a serving bowl and toss together with desired dressing. Serve at once.

PAIRING SUGGESTIONS
Salsa Verde Bean Burritos (page 122)
Salsa Verde Quinoa (page 130)

MIXED GREENS WITH CUCUMBER, CARROT & CASHEWS

It's not always easy to match a salad to Asian-flavored main dishes. This one is a good choice.

Mixed greens as desired

½ medium cucumber, quartered and sliced

1 cup or so pre-grated or petite-cut baby carrots

⅓ to ½ cup chopped toasted cashews or slivered almonds

Bottled sesame-ginger or citrus-ginger dressing

1. Combine all the ingredients in a serving bowl and toss together with desired dressing. Serve at once.

PAIRING SUGGESTIONS
Orange-Glazed Tofu (page 82)
Seitan Peppersteak (page 88)

MIXED GREENS WITH APPLE OR PEAR, AVOCADO & WALNUTS

Mixed greens team well with a touch of sweetness from fruit. This salad, which goes nicely with grain dishes, is especially tasty during the cooler months when tomatoes and other typical salad vegetables aren't as flavorful.

Mixed greens as desired

1 crisp apple or firm ripe pear, cored and diced

1 medium firm, ripe avocado

½ cup chopped walnuts

Bottled raspberry vinaigrette or French dressing

1. Combine all the ingredients in a serving bowl and toss together with desired dressing. Serve at once.

PAIRING SUGGESTIONS
Italian-Style Rice & Peas (page 136)
Farro with Mushrooms & Carrots (page 137)

MORE TIME / LESS LAZY
Make your own French Dressing (page 72).

MIXED GREENS WITH BEETS & BELL PEPPER

I love beets, but admit that I don't use them as much as I'd like. The cooking process is a tad messy and tedious. This tasty salad uses either pickled beets or the kind of prepared beets found in supermarket produce sections and natural foods stores. Love Beets™ are a popular brand. If you're using pickled beets, look for a natural brand made without high-fructose corn syrup.

Mixed greens as desired

1 (6.5-ounce) package prepared beets, sliced or 8-ounce jar sliced pickled beets, drained

1 yellow or orange bell pepper, cut into strips

¼ cup toasted sunflower seeds

Bottled balsamic vinaigrette or lemon juice and olive oil

1. Combine all the ingredients in a serving bowl and toss together with desired dressing. Serve at once.

MORE TIME / LESS LAZY
Use 2 medium beets, cooked in your preferred way, then cooled, peeled, and diced or sliced.
   Make your own **Balsamic Vinaigrette** (page 71).

PAIRING SUGGESTIONS
Cheesy Quinoa & Broccoli Skillet (page 132)
Skillet BBQ Beans & Greens (page 119)

MIXED GREENS WITH
TOMATOES, CHICKPEAS & OLIVES

This is my go-to salad to serve with meals that need a little extra protein. It's especially good with pasta dishes.

Mixed greens as desired

1 or 2 medium tomatoes, diced, or ½ pint cherry or grape tomatoes

1 (15-ounce) can chickpeas, drained and rinsed

½ cup pitted green or black olives, halved or chopped

Bottled vinaigrette, French dressing, or vegan ranch dressing

1. Combine all the ingredients in a serving bowl and toss together with desired dressing. Serve at once.

PAIRING SUGGESTIONS
Mushroom Pasta Paprikash (page 105)
Curried Greens Smashed Potatoes (page 140)

MORE TIME / LESS LAZY
Make your own **Basic Vinaigrette** (page 71), **French Dressing** (page 72), or **Vegan Ranch** (page 72) dressing.

ITALIAN TOMATO & BREAD SALAD

Juicy fresh summer tomatoes are the stars of this classic Italian salad. Crisp bread cubes and basil add an appealing flourish.

4 TO 6 SERVINGS

3 to 4 cups 1-inch Italian bread cubes, preferably whole grain

1½ to 2 pounds flavorful ripe tomatoes, diced

⅓ cup chopped pitted cured olives (such as Kalamata)

¼ cup chopped fresh basil leaves, or more to taste

2 tablespoons olive oil, preferably extra-virgin

2 tablespoons red wine vinegar

Salt and freshly ground pepper, to taste

1. Preheat the oven or toaster oven to 300°F.

2. Arrange the bread cubes on a baking sheet and bake until crisp and golden, about 15 minutes. Remove from the oven and allow to cool.

3. Combine the remaining ingredients in a serving bowl and toss together. Just before serving, stir in the bread cubes.

OPTIONAL ADDITION
✳ Add about ½ cup vegan mozzarella cheese shreds or finely diced vegan mozzarella or jack cheese.

PAIRING SUGGESTIONS
Garlicky Pasta with Zucchini (page 101)
Spinach Pesto Pasta (page 99)

WAYS TO MAKE COLESLAW

Once in a while, I enjoy using pre-cut coleslaw cabbage. It makes a big portion of salad that keeps well in the refrigerator. Coleslaw is the rare kind of salad that's good as a leftover. It's also a treat when you want something raw on the plate without chopping. Look for coleslaw that includes carrots and/or red cabbage. The cabbage should look crisp and fresh in the bag.

Of course, you can feel free to use fresh cabbage instead of the bagged coleslaw if you prefer. The recipes that follow offer both options. Simple slaws go well with many types of entrées, including bean dishes, casseroles, and vegan burgers. They're also great paired with sandwiches and wraps.

A couple of final tips: When you're making coleslaw as part of a meal, make it first to give the flavors time to blend and for the cabbage to soften. Also, try substituting broccoli slaw (also a bagged salad) for the cabbage, in whole or in part, in any of the following recipes.

CABBAGE & APPLE SLAW

This naturally sweet medley of cabbage, apples, and raisins adds crunch and eye appeal to everyday meals. It's special enough to serve at winter holiday meals, too.

6 SERVINGS

4 cups thinly shredded green cabbage or bagged coleslaw

1 medium crisp apple, any variety, cored and cut into ½-inch dice

⅓ cup raisins or dried cranberries

½ cup vegan mayonnaise, more or less as needed

Juice of ½ lemon or lime (about 2 tablespoons)

Freshly ground pepper to taste

1. Combine all the ingredients in a serving bowl and toss together well. If time allows, cover and let the slaw stand for 15 minutes or so before serving.

OPTIONAL ADDITIONS
* Add 2 large celery stalks, cut diagonally.
* Just before serving, sprinkle sunflower or pumpkin seeds on top of the slaw.

PAIRING SUGGESTIONS
Lentil Sloppy Joes (page 176)
Roasted BBQ Tempeh & Vegetables (page 90)

PINEAPPLE COLESLAW

Pineapple and pickle relish give this refreshing slaw a sweet twist, making for a nice flavor contrast with spicy and bold-flavored dishes.

6 SERVINGS

⅓ cup vegan mayonnaise

2 tablespoons sweet pickle relish

1 teaspoon yellow mustard

4 cups thinly shredded green cabbage or bagged coleslaw

½ cup finely diced (fresh or canned, well-drained) pineapple

Salt and freshly ground pepper, to taste

1. Combine the mayonnaise, relish, and mustard in a small bowl. Stir together until blended.

2. Combine the cabbage and pineapple in a serving bowl. Pour the dressing over the vegetables and stir to combine well. Season with salt and pepper.

3. If time allows, cover and let the slaw stand for 15 minutes or so before serving.

OPTIONAL ADDITIONS
* Chopped fresh parsley
* Thinly sliced scallions or minced chives
* Finely chopped red onion

PAIRING SUGGESTIONS
Zucchini & Polenta Marinara (page 148)
Seitan & Vegan Sausage with Greens (page 89)

KALE & CABBAGE SLAW

This slaw is the one I make most often, and it's absolutely addictive if you're a kale fan. It goes especially well with bean and grain dishes and is a sturdy year-round salad.

4 TO 6 SERVINGS

6 to 8 leaves curly green or lacinato kale, rinsed and dried

Olive oil, as needed

3 cups thinly shredded green or savoy cabbage, or bagged coleslaw

⅓ cup vegan mayonnaise, or as desired

Juice of ½ lemon (about 2 tablespoons), or more, to taste

½ cup grated carrots (DIY or bagged) or petite-cut baby carrots

Salt and freshly ground pepper, to taste

1. Strip the kale leaves off the stems. Slice the kale thinly and place in a serving bowl. If you'd like to use the stems, slice them thinly as well; otherwise, discard.

2. Coat your palms lightly with olive oil and massage the kale until it softens and becomes bright green, 30 to 45 seconds.

3. Add the remaining ingredients to the bowl and toss with the kale until well combined.

4. If time allows, cover and let the slaw stand for 15 minutes or so before serving.

VARIATION

✳ Replace the vegan mayo with a different salad dressing. It's fantastic with a tahini-based dressing or cilantro-lime dressing.

OPTIONAL ADDITIONS

✳ 2 to 3 tablespoons toasted sunflower seeds

✳ ¼ cup chopped fresh herb of your choice (parsley, dill, or cilantro)

PAIRING SUGGESTIONS
Crazy-Easy Sloppy Joes (page 175)
Smoky Red Beans (page 118)

CORN SLAW

Cabbage and corn team up in a slaw that goes well with Southwestern specialties and bean dishes.

6 SERVINGS

4 cups thinly shredded green cabbage or bagged coleslaw

2 cups cooked fresh or frozen corn kernels

2 scallions, thinly sliced, or ¼ cup minced fresh cilantro

½ medium red bell pepper, finely diced

½ cup bottled vinaigrette

Salt and freshly ground pepper, to taste

1. Combine all the ingredients in a serving bowl and mix together. If time allows, cover and let the slaw stand for 15 minutes or so before serving.

MORE TIME / LESS LAZY
Make your own Basic Vinaigrette (page 71).

PAIRING SUGGESTIONS
Easiest Chili Bean Tostadas (page 121)
Salsa Black Beans (page 116)

ASIAN-FLAVORED SLAW

A good addition to Asian-style meals, this slaw also pairs nicely with grain dishes and vegan burgers.

4 SERVINGS

4 cups thinly shredded napa cabbage, bagged coleslaw, or broccoli slaw

1 (15-ounce) can baby corn, drained

Chopped fresh cilantro leaves as desired

⅓ cup bottled sesame-ginger dressing

Salt and freshly ground pepper, to taste

Pumpkin or sunflower seeds for topping, as desired

1. Combine the cabbage, baby corn, and cilantro in a serving bowl and stir together.

2. Add dressing as desired (be generous, but don't drown the vegetables!).

3. Season with salt and pepper and stir again. If time allows, cover and let the slaw stand for 15 minutes or so before serving.

4. Sprinkle the pumpkin or sunflower seeds on top before serving.

PAIRING SUGGESTIONS
Lazy General Tso's Tofu (page 85)
Seitan Peppersteak (page 88)

KALE & AVOCADO SALAD

Kale and avocado are a match made in salad heaven. Half of the avocado becomes part of the dressing, and the other half provides a texture contrast with the kale. This is particularly good with tortilla specialties and bean dishes.

6 SERVINGS

1 (8- to 10-ounce) bunch curly green or lacinato kale, rinsed and dried

Olive oil, as needed

1 medium firm ripe avocado, peeled and pitted

Juice of 1 lemon or lime

1 cup petite baby carrots or pre-grated carrots

¼ cup toasted pumpkin or sunflower seeds

Salt and freshly ground pepper, to taste

1. Strip the kale leaves off the stems. Slice the kale thinly and place in a serving bowl. If you'd like to use the stems, slice them thinly as well; otherwise, discard.

2. Coat your palms lightly with olive oil and massage the kale until it softens and becomes bright green, 30 to 45 seconds.

3. Mash half of the avocado. Add it to the kale and stir to combine.

4. Finely dice the remaining avocado. Add it to the kale mixture along with the remaining ingredients and stir to combine. Serve at once.

PAIRING SUGGESTIONS
Salsa Verde Bean Burritos (page 122)
Salsa Black Beans (page 116)

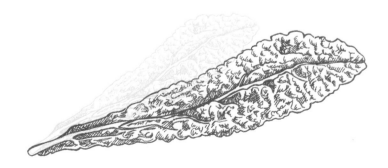

HAPPY TRAILS
KALE & APPLE SALAD

The secret to the simplicity of this massaged kale salad is using trail mix with a nice blend of nuts, seeds, and dried fruits. I've made this salad often at public food demos, and it's always devoured! The sweet aspect makes it a wonderful accompaniment to hearty and spicy dishes.

6 OR MORE SERVINGS

8 to 10 ounces kale, any variety, rinsed and dried

1 to 2 tablespoons olive oil

1 cup trail mix

1 medium apple, cored and diced

Juice of ½ to 1 lemon, to taste

1 tablespoon agave nectar

Salt and freshly ground pepper, to taste

1. Strip the kale leaves off the stems. Slice the kale thinly and place in a serving bowl. If you'd like to use the stems, slice them thinly as well; otherwise, discard.

2. Coat your palms lightly with olive oil and massage the kale until it softens and becomes bright green, 30 to 45 seconds. Add the remaining oil, along with the other ingredients, and toss to combine.

3. Taste to see if you'd like to add more lemon and/or agave for the sweet and tart balance.

4. If time allows, cover and let the salad stand for 15 minutes or so before serving.

VARIATION
✳ Use a firm ripe pear in place of the apple.

PAIRING SUGGESTIONS
Cheesy Quinoa & Broccoli Skillet (page 132)
Garlic-Herb Beans or Lentils (page 120)

TAHINI, CARROT & OLIVE SALAD

There's something delightful about contrasting the flavor of sweet carrots with briny olives. Lavished with tahini and lemon, this robust salad goes well with just about any kind of meal, and is especially compatible with bean dishes.

4 TO 6 SERVINGS

3 to 4 cups pre-grated or petite-cut baby carrots

3 tablespoons tahini (see Notes)

2 tablespoons lemon juice

½ cup green pimiento or pitted cured black olives, chopped (see Notes)

¼ cup chopped fresh dill or thinly sliced scallion

Freshly ground pepper, to taste

1. Combine the carrots, tahini, and lemon juice in a serving bowl and toss together. If the tahini clumps, gently work together with the carrots using clean hands.

2. Stir in the olives and dill. Season with pepper and serve at once.

NOTES

It's best to use tahini that's a bit runny, rather than stiff and dry. If need be, blend it in a blender or food processor with a little water to get it flowing.

To save time, you can use salad olives from a jar, which are already roughly chopped.

PAIRING SUGGESTIONS
Homemade Hummus (page 17), fresh pita, and purchased rice-stuffed grape leaves
Skillet BBQ Beans & Greens (page 119)

AVOCADO, MANGO & ARUGULA SALAD

A few well-chosen ingredients can make a huge flavor statement, proven by this combination of avocado, mango, and arugula. It's a pretty salad that brings cheer to cool-weather meals.

4 SERVINGS

1 firm ripe avocado, peeled and sliced

1 ripe mango, peeled and sliced (see Note)

Baby arugula leaves, as desired

¼ to ½ cup pecan halves or chopped walnuts, as desired

Balsamic or raspberry vinaigrette, as needed

1. Combine the avocado, mango, arugula, and pecans in a serving bowl and toss together gently.

2. Drizzle in a little dressing and toss again. Serve at once. Pass around more dressing with the salad.

NOTE
A mango can look good from the outside, but you never know what's inside—luscious, juicy flesh, or a stringy mess. Feel free to use a 12-ounce can of diced mango. Drain off the juice and use it for another purpose.

MORE TIME / LESS LAZY
Make your own **Balsamic Vinaigrette**; see the option under **Basic Vinaigrette** (page 71).

PAIRING SUGGESTION
Any of the **hot bean dishes** on pages 116 to 124.

SPINACH SALAD WITH RED CABBAGE & ORANGES

This vitamin-packed salad adds sparkling color to the plate. It's a great choice in the cooler months and is welcome with all kinds of hearty dishes.

4 TO 6 SERVINGS

4 to 6 ounces baby spinach

1½ cups thinly shredded red cabbage

3 small seedless oranges (such as clementines), peeled and sectioned

Bottled balsamic or raspberry vinaigrette, as needed

Freshly ground pepper, to taste

¼ cup toasted slivered almonds or pumpkin seeds

1. Combine the spinach, cabbage, and oranges in a serving bowl.

2. Drizzle in as much dressing as you'd like (or pass it around), grind in some pepper, and toss to combine. Scatter the almonds on top. Serve at once.

VARIATION

✳ Instead of bottled dressing, use extra-virgin olive oil and red wine vinegar. Or, if serving with an Asian-style dish, use sesame-ginger dressing.

MORE TIME / LESS LAZY
Make your own **Balsamic Vinaigrette** (page 71).

PAIRING SUGGESTIONS
Tempeh with Portobello Mushrooms (page 93)
Batter-Fried Seitan (page 87)

SPINACH SALAD WITH STRAWBERRIES & BLUEBERRIES

The classic combination of spinach and strawberries in a salad is a bit weird, but somehow it really works. I take the berry theme a bit further by adding blueberries as well, making it a perfect midsummer salad.

4 SERVINGS

2 to 3 ounces baby spinach

1 cup hulled and sliced strawberries

1 cup blueberries

⅓ chopped toasted walnuts or almonds

Citrus-ginger or raspberry vinaigrette, as needed

Freshly ground pepper, to taste

1. Combine all the ingredients in a serving bowl and toss together. Serve at once.

VARIATION

✳ Substitute arugula or mixed spring greens for the spinach.

PAIRING SUGGESTIONS
Summer Pasta with Fresh Corn & Tomatoes (page 103)
Pesto or Hummus Flatbreads (page 170)

COLD SHIRATAKI NOODLES WITH LETTUCE & SWEET CHILI SAUCE

This cold dish featuring shirataki noodles might remind you of the flavor of Asian summer rolls—without all the soaking, rolling, and fuss. Combined with crisp lettuce and bottled sweet chili sauce, it pleases the eye and the palate. Shirataki noodles come ready to use, are gluten-free, and have practically no calories. They're made with konjak yam (a tuber), and sometimes tofu is added (hence the variety called tofu shirataki), but you can get them soy-free. Look for shirataki noodles in small cellophane packages in natural foods stores and the produce department of well-stocked supermarkets.

2 TO 3 SERVINGS

1 package shirataki noodles

About half a head of romaine lettuce

¼ to ½ cup chopped fresh cilantro

¼ to ⅓ cup bottled sweet chili sauce, or as desired

Salt and freshly ground pepper, to taste

Sesame seeds or chopped peanuts, for topping

OPTIONAL ADDITIONS
* A handful of thinly sliced shiitake mushrooms
* 2 thinly sliced scallions

PAIRING SUGGESTIONS
Sweet & Savory Sautéed Tofu (page 83)
Lemon-Pepper Tofu Cutlets with Tartar Sauce (page 84)

1. Drain the noodles. Rinse them, and drain well again.

2. Slice the lettuce thinly crosswise. Combine with the shirataki noodles in a serving bowl, then add the cilantro and chili sauce.

3. With the tines of a large fork or two, toss the noodles and lettuce together.

4. Season with salt and pepper. Sprinkle the top of the salad with sesame seeds or peanuts and serve.

ZUCCHINI "NOODLES" WITH PEANUT SAUCE

This luscious dish stretches the definition of "salad," but since all the ingredients are raw, let's go for it! No spiralizer? No problem. Look for zucchini and other vegetable "noodles" in well-stocked supermarket produce sections.

4 TO 6 SERVINGS

2 medium or 4 smaller zucchini, or 10 to 12 ounces prepared zucchini noodles

2 heaping cups finely chopped broccoli florets

2 to 3 scallions, thinly sliced

1 cup bottled peanut satay sauce, or as needed

Sriracha or other hot sauce, to taste

Salt and freshly ground pepper, to taste

1. If you are preparing your own zucchini noodles, use a spiralizer with a fine or medium blade, then cut the long strands that result here and there with kitchen shears.

2. Place the zucchini noodles in a mixing bowl. Add the broccoli and scallions, then pour about half of the peanut satay sauce over the noodle mixture and toss together. Add a bit more sauce if needed to moisten the vegetables, but don't drench the dish.

3. Season the noodle dish with sriracha, to taste (or pass it around to let everyone spice their own), and salt and pepper. Let stand for a few minutes before serving. Pass around the remaining peanut satay sauce for anyone who wants more on their portion.

VARIATION

* Use a combination of the various kinds of vegetable "noodles" available in your supermarket's produce section—yellow summer squash, sweet potato, etc.

OPTIONAL ADDITIONS

* Crushed peanuts for topping
* Chopped fresh cilantro as desired

PAIRING SUGGESTIONS
Sweet & Savory Sautéed Tofu (page 83)
Tempeh Fries with Fresh Dill Mayonnaise (page 91)

TWO-BEAN SALAD

For meals that need a protein boost, such as pastas or vegetable main dishes, this salad is just the thing. It also makes a great portable lunch packed into a container for work.

4 TO 6 SERVINGS

2 (15-ounce) cans beans (two varieties; see Note), drained and rinsed

⅓ cup bottled balsamic vinaigrette dressing

¼ to ½ cup chopped fresh cilantro, parsley, or watercress leaves

2 scallions, thinly sliced

¼ cup toasted sunflower or pumpkin seeds

Salt and freshly ground pepper to taste

1. Combine all the ingredients in a serving bowl and stir together.

2. If time allows, let the salad stand for 15 minutes or more before serving to develop flavor.

NOTE
Choose two different varieties of beans; most go well together. I like combining chickpeas and pink or black beans; or cannellini (large white beans) and small red beans. The nice thing about this recipe is that you can use whatever is on hand in the pantry.

PAIRING SUGGESTIONS
Pesto & Mushroom-Stuffed Sweet Potatoes (page 146)
Summer Pasta with Fresh Corn & Tomatoes (page 103)
Greens with Polenta Wedges (page 153)

CORN & EDAMAME SALAD

Corn and edamame (fresh green soybeans) pair up to make an appealing cold dish to serve with Asian-style meals. This is especially nice with noodle dishes.

4 SERVINGS

1 cup shelled fresh or frozen edamame (fresh green soybeans)

2 to 2 ½ cups fresh corn kernels (from 2 to 3 medium ears) or thawed frozen corn

2 to 3 thinly sliced scallions

¼ cup chopped fresh cilantro, optional

¼ cup bottled vinaigrette or sesame-ginger dressing, or as needed

Salt and freshly ground pepper, to taste

1. Combine the edamame with enough water to cover in a medium saucepan. Bring to a slow boil, then lower the heat and simmer for 5 minutes. If using fresh corn, add the kernels to the saucepan with the edamame at this point and cook for 2 to 3 minutes longer, until both are just tender. Thawed frozen corn kernels can be added once the edamame are nearly tender; cook just until heated through.

2. Drain the mixture in a colander and rinse under cool running water until the vegetables stop steaming. Drain well again and transfer to a serving bowl.

3. Add the scallions, cilantro, and dressing, then season with salt and pepper. Serve at once or chill in the refrigerator until needed.

MORE TIME / LESS LAZY
Make your own Basic Vinaigrette (page 71).

PAIRING SUGGESTIONS
Streamlined Vegetable Lo Mein (page 112)
Cold Shirataki Noodles with Lettuce & Sweet Chili Sauce (page 64)

PINTO BEAN & AVOCADO SALAD

Brought to you by the Department of Yum, this lovely bean salad is richly flavored with olives and avocado.

4 SERVINGS

1 (15-ounce) can pinto beans, drained and rinsed

1 ripe avocado, diced

1 heaping cup cherry or grape tomatoes, halved

½ cup pitted black olives (halved, if large)

2 limes

Olive oil as desired, preferably extra-virgin

Salt and freshly ground pepper, to taste

1. Combine the pinto beans, avocado, tomatoes, and olives in a serving bowl. Toss together gently.

2. Add the juice of 1 lime and a drizzle of olive oil and toss again.

3. Season with salt and pepper. Cut the second lime into 4 wedges to serve with the salad.

OPTIONAL ADDITION
* Garnish each serving with a few fresh cilantro leaves.

PAIRING SUGGESTIONS
Spinach & Bell Pepper Quesadillas (page 186)
Spinach & Dill Rice (page 135)

CUCUMBER, TOMATO & CHICKPEA SALAD

Here's my go-to salad for serving with Indian-style dishes that need a protein boost. It teams nicely with other kinds of spicy dishes, too.

4 SERVINGS

½ medium cucumber, quartered lengthwise and sliced

½ pint cherry or grape tomatoes, halved

1 (15-ounce) can chickpeas, drained and rinsed

1 (6-ounce) container plain coconut yogurt (see Variation)

¼ to ½ cup chopped fresh cilantro

Salt and freshly ground pepper, to taste

1. Combine all the ingredients in a serving bowl and stir together. Serve at once.

VARIATION

✳ In place of coconut yogurt, use your favorite creamy vegan salad dressing.

PAIRING SUGGESTIONS
Curried Greens Smashed Potatoes (page 140)
Couscous Curry with Peas & Cashews (page 133)

WAYS TO MAKE SALAD DRESSING

A flavorful dressing can make any simple salad more enticing. I'm all on board with natural store-bought dressings, which are as tasty as they are convenient. Still, lazy as I can be, I often like to make my own—it's easy and economical. Here are five basic salad dressings you'll enjoy having in your repertoire.

BASIC VINAIGRETTE

This all-purpose dressing is your go-to for salads and slaws. It's also a delicious marinade for roasted vegetables, especially using the balsamic vinegar option.

MAKES ABOUT 1 CUP

½ cup extra-virgin olive oil

¼ to ⅓ cup white or red wine vinegar

1 tablespoon Dijon-style mustard

2 teaspoons natural granulated sugar or agave nectar

1 teaspoon Italian seasoning blend

1. Combine all ingredients in a bottle with a tight-fitting lid and shake thoroughly. Shake well before each use.

VARIATION

* For **Balsamic Vinaigrette**, replace the white or red wine vinegar with balsamic.

FRENCH DRESSING

This easy recipe for French dressing tastes a lot like the store-bought variety and is more economical. It's my favorite homemade dressing.

MAKES ABOUT 1 CUP

¼ cup good-quality ketchup

½ cup vegan mayonnaise

3 tablespoons olive oil

2 tablespoons red wine vinegar

1 tablespoon agave or maple syrup

½ teaspoon paprika, or more to taste

1. Combine all the ingredients in a small mixing bowl and whisk together until smoothly blended.

2. Transfer to a bottle with a tight-fitting lid. Shake well before each use.

VEGAN RANCH DRESSING

It's not easy to find bottled vegan ranch dressing, so this recipe is a must-have. You can also use it as a dip for vegetables or chips.

MAKES ABOUT 1 CUP

⅔ cup plain nondairy yogurt (6-ounce container)

¼ cup vegan mayonnaise

Juice of ½ lemon (about 2 tablespoons) or 2 tablespoons white wine vinegar

1 teaspoon salt-free seasoning blend (such as Frontier® or Mrs. Dash®)

½ teaspoon dried dill

Salt and freshly ground pepper to taste

1. Combine all the ingredients in a small bowl. Add a tablespoon or two of water and whisk together. Add a bit more water if necessary; the dressing should flow but not be runny. If you're planning to use this as a dip, omit the water.

2. Store any unused portion in an airtight container, where it will keep for several days.

THOUSAND ISLAND-ISH DRESSING

This dressing might be just the thing to inspire younger or pickier eaters to enjoy salad. It can also be used as a dip for raw vegetables or as a spread in sandwiches and wraps.

MAKES ABOUT ⅔ CUP

½ cup vegan mayonnaise

⅓ cup good-quality ketchup

½ teaspoon sweet paprika

1 tablespoon sweet pickle relish, or more to taste

1. Combine all ingredients in a small bowl and whisk together until smooth.

2. Store any unused portion in an airtight container in the refrigerator, where it will keep for several days.

GREEN GODDESS DRESSING

This strong herbal dressing, made of fresh herbs, plus tahini and cucumber, not only has a luscious taste, but makes good use of nutrient-rich parsley. Use it to your heart's content on almost any kind of salad or as a way to supercharge pre-cut coleslaw.

MAKES ABOUT 1 CUP

1 cup firmly packed fresh parsley leaves (some stems are fine)

¼ cup tahini (sesame paste)

½ cup peeled, seeded, and chopped cucumber

Juice of ½ to 1 lemon, to taste

1 to 2 tablespoons fresh dill leaves, to taste

Pinch of salt

Freshly ground pepper, to taste

1. Place all ingredients in the container of a food processor. Process until herbs are very finely minced. Transfer to a tightly lidded cruet or bottle and shake well before each use.

VARIATION

* Substitute or add other fresh summer herbs of your choice, including basil and/or oregano.

TOFU, TEMPEH & SEITAN

Tofu, tempeh, and seitan are what I like to call **"THE PROTEIN TRIO."** These non-identical triplets are the amino acid–rich building blocks of the plant-based diet—though it must be said that **BEANS ARE NO SLOUCHES** in this department.

TOFU IS A CONSTANT STAPLE in my refrigerator, with tempeh and seitan making an occasional appearance for variety. For you, it might be the opposite, or some variation, depending on which you favor. Extra-firm tofu is the most versatile in this group, followed closely by baked tofu. **TEMPEH IS MORE OF AN ACQUIRED TASTE,** with its fermented bite and grainy mouth feel. **SEITAN'S MEATY TEXTURE** is a delight to those who crave that kind of heartiness. The only caveat is that seitan is pure wheat gluten, so those with celiac or gluten sensitivity need to avoid it altogether.

The protein trio is a group of practically **READY-TO-EAT FOODS.** A good sauce, a simple preparation, and they're on the plate in no time flat.

SPINACH & MUSHROOM SCRAMBLED TOFU

Vegan tofu scrambles are easy enough to make without a recipe, so use this one as a guideline and vary it with other vegetables—tomatoes, broccoli, asparagus, or whatever happens to be in the fridge. It's the kind of dish that's welcome for any meal of the day. I prefer to use extra-firm silken tofu for scrambles, but if firm or extra-firm tofu is on hand and you're craving this kind of meal, by all means, use it. Just make sure to drain and blot it well.

2 TO 3 SERVINGS

1 to 1½ cups cleaned and sliced cremini or white mushrooms

1 (12.3-ounce) container extra-firm silken tofu, crumbled

1 teaspoon curry powder, more or less to taste

3 to 4 ounces baby spinach

¼ cup finely chopped fresh parsley or cilantro, or 2 tablespoons fresh dill

Salt (see Note) and freshly ground pepper, to taste

OPTIONAL ADDITIONS

* Nutritional yeast (highly recommended), about 2 tablespoons

* Vegan cheese shreds—about ½ cup

* Scallions—2 to 3, in addition to or instead of the fresh herbs listed

* Sriracha or other hot sauce, or dried hot red pepper flakes, to taste

COMPLETE THE MEAL

This can be the centerpiece of lunch, brunch, or dinner with whole grain toast and sliced fruit—oranges in the fall and winter, melons during the warmer months. Add some cherry or grape tomatoes. For a special occasion brunch, add **Two-Potato Hash Browns** (page 152) to the menu.

1. Combine the mushrooms in a medium skillet with a little water, cover, and cook until wilted, about 3 to 4 minutes. Drain off any liquid.

2. Crumble the tofu into the skillet and sprinkle in the curry powder. Continue to cook the mixture for about 5 minutes over medium-high heat.

3. Add the baby spinach (in batches if needed), cover, and cook briefly, just until wilted down.

4. Stir in the fresh herb of choice, season with salt and pepper, and serve at once.

NOTE

Try using *kala namak*, a Himalayan salt for an egg-like flavor and aroma.

BBQ-FLAVORED TOFU WITH ONIONS & PEPPERS

Here's an oven-roasted tofu dish that's a great go-to for cool-weather meals. It features baked tofu, a firmer, chewier cousin to the tub variety. Because it doesn't need to be drained and blotted, it saves an extra step.

4 SERVINGS

1 large onion, halved and thinly sliced, rings separated

Olive oil as needed

1 (8-ounce) package or 2 (5.5-ounce) packages baked tofu

2 bell peppers, any color

¾ cup barbecue sauce, your favorite variety, or as needed

1. Preheat the oven to 425°F.

2. Spread out the onion rings on a parchment-lined roasting pan. Drizzle them with a little olive oil and bake in the oven for 5 to 8 minutes.

3. Meanwhile, cut the tofu into bite-size dice and cut the peppers into large strips.

4. Remove the pan with the onions from the oven and stir in the tofu, peppers, and barbecue sauce.

5. Return the tofu mixture to the oven and bake for 15 minutes, then stir gently and bake for 10 minutes longer. Stir in a little more sauce if needed, then serve.

COMPLETE THE MEAL
Baked potatoes or sweet potatoes go well with this dish, and since you have the oven going at 425°F, you can get them started in the oven about 30 minutes before this dish goes in. Otherwise, hot cooked brown rice or quinoa is a good alternative. Also, consider making a batch of **Roasted Curry Cauliflower** (page 157) along with the tofu in the same oven. One of the **Coleslaw** variations on pages 52 to 57 rounds out the meal.

SOUTHWESTERN SCRAMBLED
TOFU BURRITOS

These lively scrambled tofu burritos are a nice option for a quick dinner and make an excellent weekend breakfast or brunch, too. They've been a standard of mine for years and never fail to please.

MAKES 6 BURRITOS

1 (14- to 16-ounce) tub soft or firm tofu, well drained and mashed

1 cup salsa, your favorite variety, or more, as desired

½ teaspoon curry powder

Six 8- to 10-inch soft flour tortillas

1½ cups grated vegan cheddar or pepper jack cheese

1. Cut the tofu crosswise into ½-inch-thick slices to get 6 slabs. Blot well between clean tea towels or several layers of paper towels (or use a tofu press ahead of time).

2. Mash the tofu and combine with the salsa and curry powder in a medium skillet and cook over medium heat for 7 to 8 minutes, until well heated through. Turn the heat up and cook a little longer if there's any excess liquid in the skillet.

3. Divide the scrambled tofu mixture among the tortillas, placing it in the centers and leaving room at each end. Divide the vegan cheese evenly over the tortillas.

4. Microwave each tortilla for 30 to 40 seconds, or until the cheese is melted. Fold in the two ends over the tofu mixture, then roll up the tortilla. Repeat with each tortilla, then serve the burritos at once.

COMPLETE THE MEAL
For brunch, add **Super-Easy Guacamole** (page 22; or store-bought), chips, and some fresh fruit—orange and grapefruit in the winter, and melons when it's warmer. For dinner, serve with baked or microwaved potatoes or sweet potatoes, too.

TOFU & GREEN BEANS TERIYAKI

Preparing this almost mindlessly easy tofu teriyaki might make you feel like a bit of a slacker, but when you serve it, you'll get nothing but compliments.

3 TO 4 SERVINGS

1 (8-ounce) package (or two 5.5-ounce packages) baked tofu

1 (16-ounce) bag frozen whole green beans, preferably organic, thawed

½ cup bottled teriyaki marinade, or as needed

3 to 4 scallions, sliced

Sriracha or other hot seasoning

1. Cut the tofu into strips or dice.

2. Combine the tofu and green beans in a stir-fry pan or large skillet with the teriyaki marinade. Cook over high heat, stirring often, until the green beans are tender-crisp, about 8 minutes.

3. Stir in the scallions and taste to see if you'd like to add more teriyaki marinade.

4. Season with sriracha (or pass around for everyone to spice up as they'd like). Serve at once.

COMPLETE THE MEAL

About that sushi in the photo—of course, we're not going to make it from scratch. Many large supermarkets (as well as natural foods markets) sell freshly made sushi rolls, so for convenience, you can pick them up while getting the other ingredients. As an alternative to sushi, you can serve this meal with vegetable spring rolls or dumplings from the frozen foods section. If you want to skip these add-ons, you might consider **Hoisin-Glazed Eggplant** (page 165). With any of these options, add a platter of cherry tomatoes and sliced bell peppers.

MORE TIME / LESS LAZY

For the one or two months of the year when good organic green beans are available, by all means, use them. It takes a bit of patience to cut the tips from a pound of green beans, but when they're in season, it's worth it!

ORANGE-GLAZED TOFU

Fruit preserves, orange juice, and soy sauce create a luscious glaze for tofu with no added fat. Consider doubling this recipe if you're feeding tofu fans—it's addictive!

3 TO 4 SERVINGS

1 (14- to 16-ounce) tub extra-firm tofu

¼ cup apricot or peach preserves, or orange marmalade

¼ cup orange juice (fresh-squeezed or bottled)

2 tablespoons soy sauce or tamari

2 teaspoons grated fresh or jarred ginger

1. Cut the tofu crosswise into ½-inch-thick slices to get 6 slabs. Blot well between clean tea towels or several layers of paper towels (or use a tofu press ahead of time), then cut each slab in half to get 12 little squares of tofu.

2. Combine the preserves, orange juice, soy sauce, and ginger in a small bowl and whisk together.

3. Set a medium skillet over medium heat and pour in the preserves mixture. When it starts bubbling, arrange the tofu over it in a single layer. Turn the heat up to medium-high and cook each side for 5 minutes, or until the tofu is nicely glazed and most of the liquid has been absorbed.

4. Serve at once, scooping up any remaining glaze to top the tofu pieces.

OPTIONAL ADDITIONS
* Thinly sliced scallions for garnish
* Black or white sesame seeds for garnish

COMPLETE THE MEAL
For a yummy dinner, serve with **Chinese-Style Riced Cauliflower** (page 156) or **Braised Bok Choy with Shiitake Mushrooms** (page 154) and **Asian-Flavored Slaw** (page 57).

SWEET & SAVORY SAUTÉED TOFU

When I want a basic tofu dish to boost the protein content of a meal, I most often turn to this one. My kids cut their teeth on it (though you really can't cut your teeth on tofu, can you?) and it continues to be a favorite.

2 TO 3 SERVINGS

1 (14- to 16-ounce) tub extra-firm tofu

1 tablespoon neutral vegetable oil

1 tablespoon maple syrup or agave,
   or as needed

1 tablespoon soy sauce or tamari,
   or as needed

OPTIONAL ADDITIONS

* 1 cup or so grated or petite-cut baby carrots, stirred in once the tofu is almost done

* 2 to 3 slices scallion, stirred in once the tofu is almost done

* Sriracha or other hot sauce—season to taste once the tofu is done, or pass around

COMPLETE THE MEAL

Serve this tofu preparation with **Chinese-Style Riced Cauliflower (page 156)** or **Streamlined Vegetable Lo Mein (page 112)**. Or, serve it with **Braised Bok Choy with Shiitake Mushrooms (page 154)** and brown rice.

1. Cut the tofu crosswise into ½-inch-thick slices to get 6 slabs. Blot well between clean tea towels or several layers of paper towels (or use a tofu press ahead of time), then cut each slab into dice.

2. Slowly heat the oil, 1 tablespoon maple syrup, and 1 tablespoon soy sauce together in a skillet or stir-fry pan, stirring constantly as the mixture warms and comes together as a glaze.

3. Add the tofu and stir quickly to coat it with the glaze, then continue to sauté over medium-high heat until golden-brown and crisp on most sides, about 10 minutes. Taste and add more syrup and/or soy sauce if you'd like.

LEMON-PEPPER TOFU CUTLETS
WITH TARTAR SAUCE

You'll want to double this simple yet elegant tofu recipe if you're serving more than two, because everyone will want two pieces.

2 SERVINGS

1 (14- to 16-ounce) tub extra-firm tofu

Juice of 1 lemon (about ¼ cup)

1 tablespoon safflower or olive oil

¼ teaspoon salt

Freshly ground pepper

FOR THE VEGAN TARTAR SAUCE

½ cup vegan mayonnaise

1 tablespoon sweet pickle relish

1 to 2 teaspoons yellow mustard, or to taste

1. Cut the tofu in half crosswise, then cut each half in the other direction to make 4 slabs. Blot very well with clean tea towels or several layers of paper towels (or use a tofu press ahead of time).

2. Combine the lemon juice, oil, salt, and lots of pepper in a medium skillet. Arrange the tofu cutlets in the skillet in a single layer and cook over medium-high heat for 5 minutes. Carefully flip the cutlets over and continue to cook until the tofu absorbs all the marinade. Flip the cutlets and cook again on both sides until they are golden brown.

3. Meanwhile, make the tartar sauce: Combine all the ingredients for the tartar sauce in a small bowl and stir together until well blended. Pass around for topping the tofu.

COMPLETE THE MEAL
This is lovely with **Couscous Curry with Peas & Cashews** (page 133), **Greens with Polenta Wedges** (page 153), or **Stir-Fried Collards & Carrots** (page 160).

LAZY GENERAL TSO'S TOFU

It's fun to try to recreate favorite restaurant dishes at home, and General Tso's Tofu has long been a family standard. The secret to General Tso's is in the sauce, and I could never quite get the right balance of sweet, tangy, and spicy flavors. A lot of ingredients are involved! Fortunately, excellent General Tso's sauce is now available in the Asian foods section of well-stocked supermarkets.

3 TO 4 SERVINGS

1 (14- to 16-ounce) tub extra-firm tofu

1 tablespoon neutral vegetable oil, such as safflower

1 large or two medium broccoli crowns

¾ cup bottled General Tso's sauce, more or less as needed

1. Cut the tofu crosswise into ½-inch-thick slices to get 6 slabs. Blot well between clean tea towels or several layers of paper towel (or use a tofu press ahead of time). Cut each slab into dice.

2. Heat the oil in a large skillet or stir-fry pan. Add the tofu and sauté over medium-high heat about 8 to 10 minutes, stirring often, until golden and crisp on most sides. Transfer the tofu to a plate or bowl. Set aside.

3. Cut the broccoli into bite-size florets and steam in the same skillet with about ½ inch of water until tender-crisp, then drain off any remaining liquid.

4. Gently stir the tofu back into the skillet with the broccoli, then add enough of the General Tso's sauce to generously coat the tofu and broccoli. Continue to cook the mixture over medium heat until heated through, then serve at once.

OPTIONAL ADDITIONS

* Traditionally, General Tso's tofu comes with small, fresh, hot red chile peppers, which are on the incendiary side of the heat scale. Add a few of them if you can stand the heat! Or, you can add milder chile peppers if you'd like.

* Though I've never seen scallions in General Tso's Tofu, it definitely doesn't hurt to add a couple of thinly sliced scallions when you stir in the bottled sauce.

COMPLETE THE MEAL

Serve this tofu dish with brown rice or any kind of noodle—soba, udon, or even spaghetti. **Spinach Salad with Red Cabbage & Oranges** (page 62) adds color to the plate; **Asian-Flavored Slaw** (57) is a good choice as well. Frozen vegetable spring rolls are a fun but totally optional addition to the meal; follow the package instructions for warming them up.

PEANUT SATAY TOFU TRIANGLES

Cutting tofu into triangles doesn't make it taste any different, but the shape gives it more eye appeal. Look for peanut satay sauce in the Asian foods section of well-stocked supermarkets or natural foods stores.

3 TO 4 SERVINGS

1 (14- to 16-ounce) tub extra-firm tofu

1 tablespoon safflower or other high-heat vegetable oil

1 tablespoon soy sauce or tamari

½ cup bottled peanut satay sauce, plus more for serving

½ teaspoon sriracha or other hot sauce

Shredded crisp lettuce or napa cabbage, as needed, for serving

OPTIONAL ADDITION

✳ Sprinkle the tofu triangles with dried hot red pepper flakes once they're arranged on the platter.

COMPLETE THE MEAL

Add hot cooked rice, noodles, or rice vermicelli to this meal. A steamed green vegetable, like broccoli or asparagus, is a nice addition, too. Or, if you want to go a step further with a nutritious vegetable dish, **Stir-Fried Collards & Carrots** (page 160) or **Spicy Walnut Green Beans** (page 164) are great options. Add a platter of cherry tomatoes and baby carrots.

1. Cut each block of tofu crosswise into 6 slabs. Blot well between clean tea towels or several layers of paper towels (or use a tofu press ahead of time). Cut each slab in half to make 2 squares. Finally, cut each square on the diagonal to make triangles.

2. Heat the oil and soy sauce in a wide skillet. Arrange the tofu triangles in a single layer in the mixture and sauté, in batches if needed, over medium-high heat until golden on both sides.

3. Drizzle the satay sauce and sriracha over the tofu triangles in the skillet. Stir gently, turning them over a few times, until nicely glazed.

4. To serve, line a platter with the shredded lettuce and arrange the tofu triangles over it.

5. Serve at once, passing around the bottle of peanut satay sauce and extra sriracha for those who would like more.

BATTER-FRIED SEITAN

Seitan cooked in a batter until crisp may not be the prettiest dish ever, but I can almost guarantee that it will disappear quickly.

4 SERVINGS

¼ cup fine cornmeal or chickpea flour

¾ cup boiling water

¼ cup whole-wheat pastry flour

1½ teaspoons salt-free seasoning blend

¼ teaspoon salt

16 ounces seitan, cut into thin strips or bite-size chunks

2 tablespoons safflower or other high-heat vegetable oil

1. Combine the cornmeal and water in a mixing bowl. Let stand for 1 minute, then stir. Add the flour, seasoning blend, and salt, and whisk together to make a thick batter.

2. Add the seitan to the batter, then stir to coat it evenly.

3. Heat the oil in a wide skillet. Arrange the seitan in the skillet in a single layer (or cook in batches if needed) and sauté over medium-high heat, turning frequently, until the batter turns golden brown and crusty on most sides. Serve at once.

OPTIONAL ADDITION

* Add a tablespoon or two of nutritional yeast to the batter for a nice flavor boost.

COMPLETE THE MEAL

Add color to the plate with **Spinach Salad with Red Cabbage & Oranges** (page 62) and microwaved or baked sweet potatoes. Another option is to serve this with **Stir-Fried Greens & Napa Cabbage** (page 161) and a bowl of red and yellow cherry tomatoes.

SEITAN PEPPERSTEAK

Here's a simplified and veganized version of a Chinese restaurant classic with hearty seitan stealing the show.

4 SERVINGS

- 2 tablespoons safflower or other neutral oil
- 1 large red or yellow onion, quartered and thinly sliced
- 2 medium bell peppers, any color (or two different colors), cut into narrow strips
- 12 to 16 ounces seitan, cut into bite-size strips
- ⅓ to ½ cup teriyaki marinade, plus more as needed
- Freshly ground pepper, to taste

1. Heat 1 tablespoon oil in a wide skillet or stir-fry pan. Add the onion and sauté over medium-low heat until translucent. Add the bell peppers, then turn up the heat and continue to cook the vegetables, stirring often, until lightly browned. Transfer to a dish and set aside.

2. Heat the remaining tablespoon of oil in the skillet. Add the seitan and sauté over medium-high heat, stirring often, until golden brown on most sides. Pour in half of the teriyaki marinade, reduce the heat, and cook for a minute or so longer, until the seitan is nicely glazed.

3. Stir in the onion and peppers mixture, season with pepper. Finish with enough additional teriyaki marinade to coat everything nicely. Serve at once.

OPTIONAL ADDITIONS

* Add 2 to 3 cloves chopped garlic when adding the bell peppers.
* Add a teaspoon or two of grated fresh ginger at the same time as the marinade.
* Add dried hot red pepper flakes or sriracha to taste to the final dish, or pass the sriracha around.

COMPLETE THE MEAL

Brown rice is always a welcome accompaniment, as are rice vermicelli or bean-thread noodles. A platter of cherry tomatoes, sliced cucumbers, and carrots rounds out the meal. For a heftier meal, you can also add **Spicy Walnut Green Beans** (page 164) or **Spicy Sesame Broccoli** (page 167).

SEITAN & VEGAN SAUSAGE WITH GREENS

Vegan sausages are a protein source that provides spice and texture to a meal. I prefer Tofurky® or Field Roast® brands, since they're made with tofu and seitan, rather than processed soy protein. Their bold flavor is a perfect foil for fresh greens.

4 TO 6 SERVINGS

1½ tablespoons olive oil

4 to 5 cloves garlic, minced

1 (8-ounce) package seitan, cut into bite-size chunks

1 (14-ounce) package vegan sausage, any variety, sliced ½-inch thick

1 (8- to 12-ounce) bunch green chard or kale

1 to 2 teaspoons salt-free seasoning blend, to taste

Salt and freshly ground pepper, to taste

VARIATION

✳ Replace the water used to steam the greens with dry white wine if you happen to have a bottle open.

COMPLETE THE MEAL

This robust main dish can be served simply with a hot cooked grain or baked or microwaved potatoes or sweet potatoes. Go a step further with **Smashed Potatoes with Mushroom Gravy** (page 141). A salad with a fruity twist, like **Cabbage & Apple Slaw** (page 53), is a nice touch.

1. Heat the oil in a stir-fry pan or wide skillet. Add the garlic, seitan, and sausage, and sauté over medium-low heat, stirring often, until the mixture is golden.

2. Meanwhile, trim the greens away from their stems and chop into bite-size pieces. Slice the stems thinly. Rinse the greens and stems well.

3. Add the greens and stems to the pan with about ¼ cup water (just enough to keep the pan moist). Cover and cook for 5 to 7 minutes, stirring occasionally, or until the greens are cooked to your liking but stay bright green.

4. Season with the seasoning blend, salt, and pepper. Serve at once.

ROASTED BBQ TEMPEH & VEGETABLES

Tempeh fans will appreciate this hearty barbecue-flavored preparation that makes a satisfying weeknight meal.

6 SERVINGS

2 (8-ounce) packages tempeh

2 bell peppers, cut into wide strips

1 medium onion, halved and thinly sliced, rings separated

¾ cup natural barbecue sauce, or more as needed

1 medium zucchini, sliced ¼-inch thick

1. Preheat the oven to 425°F.

2. Cut the tempeh into ½-inch strips.

3. Combine the tempeh with the peppers, onion, and barbecue sauce in a mixing bowl. Stir together, then transfer to a lightly oiled or parchment-lined roasting pan.

4. Bake the tempeh mixture for 10 minutes. Stir in the zucchini and bake for 15 to 20 minutes longer, or until the tempeh and vegetables are nicely roasted.

VARIATIONS

* Use 8 to 10 ounces brown mushrooms, cleaned and stemmed, in place of the zucchini.

* Use a smallish eggplant in place of the zucchini.

COMPLETE THE MEAL
Round the meal out simply with cooked brown rice (or go a step further with **Spinach & Dill Rice**, page 135), couscous or quinoa, and a colorful mixed greens salad. Since the oven temperature is already at 425°F, consider making a batch of **Roasted Curry Cauliflower** (page 157) at the same time.

TEMPEH FRIES WITH FRESH DILL MAYONNAISE

If your meal needs some extra protein to bolster a light grain or pasta entrée, this is a nice choice. It also works well as an appetizer. These can be a bit addictive, so consider doubling the recipe if you're preparing it for hungry tempeh fans.

4 SERVINGS

1 (8-ounce) package tempeh (any variety)

1 tablespoon olive oil

2 tablespoons soy sauce or tamari

FRESH DILL MAYONNAISE

¼ cup vegan mayonnaise

2 to 3 teaspoons lemon or lime juice, to taste

¼ cup minced fresh dill

Freshly ground pepper, to taste

1. Cut the block of tempeh crosswise into ½-inch-thick strips.

2. Heat the oil and soy sauce in a wide skillet. Add the tempeh, stirring quickly to coat, and sauté over medium-high heat, stirring gently and frequently, until golden and crisp on most sides, about 10 minutes.

3. Meanwhile, make the fresh dill mayonnaise: Combine the mayonnaise and lemon juice in a small serving bowl and whisk together until smooth. Stir in the dill. Season with pepper.

4. Once the fries are done, remove them from the skillet and arrange on a platter. Serve at once with the dill mayonnaise.

COMPLETE THE MEAL
Serve the fries with a light pasta dish like **Spinach Pesto Pasta** (page 99), **Pasta with Broccoli & Sun-Dried Tomatoes** (page 102), or **Garlicky Pasta with Zucchini** (page 101). Or another nice pairing is **Coconut Creamed Corn** (page 163). With any of these options, add a simple mixed greens salad.

SWEET & SMOKY TEMPEH STRIPS

Mildly sweet, salty, and smoky, these tempeh strips are delightful served on the side of a plate or as part of a vegan BLT sandwich. They go especially well with pasta and grain dishes.

4 SERVINGS

1 (8-ounce) package tempeh

2 tablespoons soy sauce or tamari

2 tablespoons good-quality ketchup

2 tablespoons maple syrup

1 tablespoon olive oil

1 to 2 teaspoons barbecue seasoning such as mesquite or smoky maple, to taste

1. Cut the block of tempeh crosswise into ¼-inch-thick strips.

2. Combine the soy sauce, ketchup, syrup, and oil in a small bowl and stir together.

3. Heat the soy sauce and ketchup mixture in a wide skillet. Arrange the tempeh strips over the sauce, cover to prevent splattering, and cook over medium-low heat on both sides until the sauce is absorbed and the tempeh starts to brown lightly.

4. Sprinkle in the barbecue seasoning, stir to distribute evenly, and cook for another minute or so. Serve warm or at room temperature as suggested in the headnote.

NOTE

Barbecue seasoning is available in the spice section of supermarkets. Try mesquite or smoky maple flavors for this recipe.

OPTIONAL ADDITION

✳ To make spicy strips, add sriracha or other hot sauce to taste to the soy sauce and ketchup mixture. You can also just pass sriracha around for spicing up individual servings.

COMPLETE THE MEAL

Like Tempeh Fries, Sweet & Smoky Tempeh Strips complement light pasta dishes. See the menu suggestions under **Tempeh Fries with Fresh Dill Mayonnaise** (page 91). You can also pair this recipe with **Quinoa with Cauliflower & Cranberries** (page 128).

TEMPEH WITH PORTOBELLO MUSHROOMS

Here tempeh and portobello mushrooms are combined to make a "meaty" meatless dish. A bottled Asian sauce adds a superb flavor boost to meld the ingredients.

4 SERVINGS

2 tablespoons olive oil

1 (8-ounce) package tempeh (any variety), sliced ¼-inch thick

1 medium onion, halved and sliced

3 to 4 portobello mushrooms, cleaned, stemmed, and sliced

½ cup bottled General Tso's or teriyaki marinade, or as needed

Freshly ground pepper, to taste

¼ cup chopped fresh parsley or sliced scallion, or more, as desired

1. Heat half of the oil in a wide skillet. Add the tempeh and cook over medium-high heat on both sides until golden brown. Remove from the skillet.

2. Heat the remaining oil in the same skillet. Add the onions and sauté over medium heat until golden. Add the sliced mushrooms and continue to sauté, stirring often, until lightly browned.

3. Return the tempeh to the pan. Add enough bottled sauce to coat everything nicely and continue to cook for 2 to 3 minutes longer.

4. Season with pepper, stir in the parsley, and serve.

COMPLETE THE MEAL
Serve the dish with a simple cooked grain—brown rice, quinoa, or couscous—and a colorful green salad or **Spinach Salad with Red Cabbage & Oranges** (page 62).

5

PASTA & NOODLES

When was the last time you heard anyone say "I don't like pasta"? This **CROWD-PLEASING PANTRY STAPLE** is a boon to gourmands, fussy eaters, and kids alike. Inexpensive and versatile, pasta and noodles are **UNDENIABLY COMFORTING**, surprisingly nourishing staples. To get off the beaten path with imported **PASTAS FROM ITALY** or with **ASIAN NOODLES** like udon and soba, you no longer have to scour specialty stores because most well-stocked supermarkets carry them. And, not to leave anyone out, **GLUTEN-FREE OPTIONS** have expanded as well and are readily available.

In the time it takes to cook almost any kind of pasta or noodle, a few fresh vegetables and a tasty sauce can be prepared to embellish them. Usually, all you'll need is a streamlined salad to complete a **SATISFYING MEAL**.

VEGAN RAVIOLI
WITH PINK BEANS

This dish has all the earmarks of an emergency dinner, but no one will be the wiser once it's sitting elegantly on the plate! Look for vegan ravioli in the refrigerator section of natural foods stores and well-stocked supermarkets.

2 TO 3 SERVINGS

1 (8- to 12-ounce) package vegan ravioli

1 tablespoon olive oil

3 to 4 cloves garlic, finely chopped

1 (15-ounce) can pink beans, drained and rinsed

1½ cups marinara sauce (use a chunky variety)

5 to 6 ounces baby spinach, rinsed

Salt and freshly ground pepper, to taste

1. Cook the ravioli according to the package directions, then drain.

2. Meanwhile, heat the oil in a stir-fry pan or large skillet. Add the garlic and sauté for a minute or two over medium-low heat. Add the beans and marinara sauce and bring to a gentle simmer. Add the spinach, cover, and cook until just wilted.

3. Gently stir in the cooked ravioli. Season with salt and pepper (you may not need salt; taste before adding). Serve at once.

OPTIONAL ADDITIONS
Top each serving with any of the following:

* Sliced fresh basil leaves or chopped fresh parsley

* Nutritional yeast or **Easiest Vegan Parmesan-Style Topping** (page 113)

* Dried hot red pepper flakes, to taste

COMPLETE THE MEAL
Serve with **Mixed Greens with Apple or Pear, Avocado & Walnuts** (page 47) for a nice flavor contrast. Add fresh olive bread if you'd like to give more heft to the meal.

EGGPLANT & GARLIC PASTA

Many classic Italian dishes are straightforward as well as appealing. This basic version of *pasta alla Norma* features eggplant and lots of garlic. In the time it takes to boil the water and cook the pasta, the sauce can be made from start to finish. Be generous with the red pepper flakes if you like a little spice—they give the dish a nice heat.

6 SERVINGS

10 to 12 ounces pasta (any short chunky shape, like rotini)

1 medium-large or 2 medium eggplants

2 tablespoons olive oil, preferably extra-virgin

4 to 6 cloves garlic, minced

1 (28-ounce) jar marinara sauce (use a full-flavored, chunky variety)

Salt and freshly ground pepper, to taste

Sliced fresh basil or chopped fresh parsley, as desired

1. Cook the pasta according to the package directions until al dente, then drain and return to the pot.

2. Cut the eggplant crosswise into ¾-inch-thick slices, then into large dice.

3. Meanwhile, heat the oil in a stir-fry pan or large skillet. Add the garlic and sauté over medium-low heat until golden. Add the eggplant and ½ cup water and cook over medium heat, stirring occasionally, until just tender. Stir in the marinara sauce and cook over medium heat until piping hot.

4. Combine the eggplant mixture with the cooked pasta in the pot and stir together. Season with salt and pepper, then stir in as much fresh basil as you'd like. Serve at once.

OPTIONAL ADDITIONS
Top with any of the following:

* Fresh basil leaves, whole or sliced, as desired

* Nutritional yeast or **Easiest Vegan Parmesan-Style Topping** (page 113)

* Dried hot red pepper flakes, to taste

COMPLETE THE MEAL
Add extra protein to the plate with **Two-Bean Salad** (page 66) or **Pinto Bean & Avocado Salad** (page 68).

PASTA WITH CREAMY ALFREDO SAUCE

Here's a mild and creamy Alfredo-style sauce with a fraction of the fat and calories of the traditional cream-based version. Kids and adults alike will enjoy this comforting cousin of mac and cheese!

4 TO 6 SERVINGS

12 ounces pasta (your favorite long or short shape)

2 tablespoons vegan butter

2 to 3 cloves garlic, minced

1 (12.3-ounce) container silken tofu

½ cup unsweetened nondairy milk

1 teaspoon salt, or to taste

Freshly ground pepper, to taste

1. Cook the pasta according to the package directions until al dente, then drain. Combine the cooked pasta and half of the vegan butter in a serving bowl and toss together.

2. Meanwhile, heat the remaining vegan butter in a small skillet. Add the garlic and sauté over low heat for 2 to 3 minutes until golden.

3. Combine the sautéed garlic with the tofu, nondairy milk, and salt in a food processor. Process until completely smooth and creamy.

4. Stir the sauce with the cooked pasta until evenly coated. Season with pepper. Taste to see if you'd like to add more salt, then serve.

TIP

If you have leftovers of this dish, you may need to add a bit more nondairy milk when reheating.

OPTIONAL ADDITIONS

Stir either or both of the following into the finished dish:

* Wilted mushrooms
* Wilted baby spinach

COMPLETE THE MEAL

Serve with sautéed or steamed broccoli or green beans and **Mixed Greens with Tomatoes, Chickpeas & Olives** (page 49).

SPINACH PESTO PASTA

Spinach with lots of parsley makes a less intensely flavored pesto sauce than the traditional recipe made with basil. The advantage is that it stays greener (basil tends to brown quickly) and keeps longer than basil pesto. And honestly, it's just as tasty.

4 TO 6 SERVINGS

10 to 12 ounces pasta (your favorite long or short shape)

FOR THE PESTO

2 tablespoons olive oil, preferably extra-virgin

3 to 4 cloves garlic, chopped

Juice of ½ lemon, plus more to taste if needed

5 to 6 ounces baby spinach, rinsed

½ cup firmly packed parsley leaves (some stem is fine)

Salt and freshly ground pepper, to taste

MAKE THE PASTA

1. Cook the pasta according to the package directions until al dente, then drain and transfer to a serving bowl.

MAKE THE PESTO

1. Heat half of the oil in a small skillet. Add the garlic and sauté for a minute or two over low heat until golden. Combine the sautéed garlic with the lemon juice, spinach (in batches if needed), and parsley in a food processor. Pulse until the mixture is coarsely and evenly pureed. Drizzle in a little water to keep the mixture moving.

2. Stir the pesto into the cooked pasta along with the remaining olive oil. Season with salt and pepper, then taste to see if you'd like to add more lemon juice. Serve warm or at room temperature.

VARIATION

✳ When basil is plentiful (big bunches tend to be expensive out of season), feel free to use it instead of the parsley, or in combination with it.

OPTIONAL ADDITIONS

✳ For a richer pesto, add ½ cup chopped walnuts to the food processor with the other ingredients.

✳ Top with nutritional yeast or **Easiest Vegan Parmesan-Style Topping** (page 113).

COMPLETE THE MEAL

This is delightful with **Italian Tomato & Bread Salad** (page 50) and **Garlic-Herb Beans or Lentils** (page 120).

PASTA WITH POWER GREENS
OR BROCCOLI SLAW

If you like your pasta with lots of veggies but don't love chopping, bagged power greens or broccoli slaw provide a handy shortcut. The power greens blend I get at my local supermarket contains chopped brussels sprouts, napa cabbage, kohlrabi, broccoli, carrots, and kale. Broccoli slaw doesn't contain quite as much variety of vegetables, but works well, too. A generous amount of garlic and sun-dried tomatoes infuse this dish with plenty of flavor.

6 OR MORE SERVINGS

16 ounces pasta (any short shape, try a tricolor variety for eye appeal)

2 tablespoons olive oil, preferably extra-virgin

3 to 4 cloves garlic, finely chopped

1 (10- to 12-ounce) package power greens or broccoli slaw

½ cup sliced sun-dried tomatoes (see Note)

Dried hot red pepper flakes, to taste

Salt and freshly ground pepper, to taste

1. Cook the pasta according to the package directions until al dente, then drain and transfer to a large serving bowl.

2. Meanwhile, heat the oil in a large skillet or stir-fry pan. Add the garlic and sauté over low heat for a minute or two, until golden. Add the greens and just enough water to keep the pan moist. Cover and cook, stirring occasionally, about 5 to 7 minutes, until tender-crisp.

3. Combine the greens mixture and sun-dried tomatoes with the cooked pasta and toss together. Season with red pepper flakes, salt, and pepper. Serve at once.

NOTE
Use dried tomatoes that are nice and moist, or oil-packed, as you prefer.

OPTIONAL ADDITIONS
Top the pasta with either or both of the following:

* Chopped fresh parsley or sliced fresh basil, as desired

* Nutritional yeast or **Easiest Vegan Parmesan-Style Topping** (page 113)

COMPLETE THE MEAL
Serve with a simple **Mixed Greens Salad** (or choose from the ones on pages 44 to 49) and **Smoky Red Beans** (page 118).

GARLICKY PASTA WITH ZUCCHINI

This version of *pasta aglia olio* (pasta with garlic and olive oil) is an Italian classic that's welcome any time you crave a light yet satisfying pasta dish. It's especially good when small zucchini come to market in midsummer.

6 OR MORE SERVINGS

16 ounces spaghetti (or other long pasta)

2 medium or 4 small zucchini (about 1 pound), sliced

3 tablespoons olive oil, preferably extra-virgin

6 cloves garlic, finely chopped

¼ cup dry white wine

Sliced fresh basil leaves or chopped parsley, as desired

Salt and freshly ground pepper, to taste

1. Cook the pasta according to the package directions until al dente, then drain and transfer to a large serving bowl.

2. Meanwhile, if using medium zucchini, quarter them lengthwise, then slice about ¼ inch thick. If using small zucchini, slice into ¼-inch-thick rounds.

3. Heat half of the oil in a large wide skillet. Add the garlic and sauté over low heat for a minute or two. Stir in the zucchini slices and add the wine. Raise the heat to medium, then cover and cook until just tender-crisp.

4. Combine the zucchini mixture with the cooked pasta. Stir in the remaining oil and the basil. Season with salt and pepper and serve.

VARIATION

✳ Use yellow summer squash or pattypan squash, especially in season.

OPTIONAL ADDITIONS
Top individual portions of pasta with any one or two of the following:

✳ Sliced sun-dried tomatoes

✳ Chopped black olives

✳ Toasted pine nuts or chopped walnuts

✳ Easiest Vegan Parmesan-Style Topping (page 113), as desired

✳ Nutritional yeast, as desired

COMPLETE THE MEAL
Like a number of the other lighter pasta dishes in this chapter, this one goes well with **Mixed Greens with Tomatoes, Chickpeas & Olives** (page 49). Add another green vegetable to the plate if you'd like—wilted greens, green beans, or asparagus.

PASTA WITH BROCCOLI &
SUN-DRIED TOMATOES

This pasta dish is nothing fancy, but it's long been a standard in my kitchen. Making generous use of broccoli, one of my family's favorite vegetables, it's become one of my comfort classics.

4 TO 6 SERVINGS

10 to 12 ounces pasta (any short chunky shape)

2 tablespoons olive oil, preferably extra-virgin

3 to 4 cloves garlic, minced

2 to 3 good-size broccoli crowns, cut into bite-size pieces

½ to ⅔ cup sliced sun-dried tomatoes (see Note)

Salt and freshly ground pepper, to taste

Dried hot red pepper flakes, to taste

1. Cook the pasta according to the package directions until al dente, then drain and transfer to a large serving bowl.

2. Meanwhile, heat the oil in a large skillet. Add the garlic and sauté for a minute or two over low heat, just until golden. Add the broccoli to the skillet along with about ¼ cup water to keep the pan moist. Cover and steam over medium heat until the broccoli is bright green and just a little beyond tender-crisp. Remove from the heat.

3. Combine the cooked pasta with the broccoli mixture (along with any liquid remaining in the pan). Add the dried tomatoes and toss together. Season with salt, pepper, and red pepper flakes. Serve at once.

NOTE
Since sun-dried tomatoes are used generously in this dish, you might consider using ones that are nice and moist but not oil-cured, but that's entirely your choice.

COMPLETE THE MEAL
Serve with **Pinto Bean & Avocado Salad** (page 68). Add fresh olive bread for a special treat.

SUMMER PASTA WITH FRESH CORN & TOMATOES

This tasty pasta dish is a perfect way to use fresh summer corn and tomatoes when they're at their peak of flavor and abundance. I especially like this with spelt or quinoa ribbon noodles, but any short chunky pasta shape will work.

6 SERVINGS

10 to 12 ounces pasta (any short chunky shape)

2 tablespoons olive oil, preferably extra-virgin

1 large onion, chopped

3 to 4 cups fresh corn kernels (from 4 medium ears)

4 to 5 ripe juicy tomatoes, diced

¼ to ½ cup chopped fresh parsley or sliced basil

Salt and freshly ground pepper, to taste

1. Cook the pasta according to the package directions until al dente, then drain and transfer to a serving bowl.

2. Meanwhile, heat the oil in a large skillet or stir-fry pan. Add the onions and sauté over low heat until golden. Add the corn kernels and a little water to the pan. Cook until the corn is tender-crisp, about 3 to 4 minutes. Add the tomatoes and cook until they start to soften, about 3 to 4 minutes.

3. Combine the corn and tomato mixture with the cooked pasta and toss to combine. Stir in the parsley, season with salt and lots of pepper, and serve.

COMPLETE THE MEAL
Push the summer theme to its fullest by serving this dish with **Spinach Salad with Strawberries & Blueberries** (page 63) and sautéed summer squashes.

MAC & CHEESE WITH SECRET CAULIFLOWER SAUCE

I usually make my simple vegan mac and cheese with silken tofu, but not long ago, the craving hit when there was no silken tofu in the pantry. Luckily, I had the brainstorm to make the sauce with some cauliflower that was on hand, and it worked like a charm. When it comes to kids (or fussy eaters), I've always found that it's always better to try to get them to love veggies rather than to disguise them. But if you're dealing with hopeless cases, this form of subterfuge can go a long way. If you're already a veggie lover, you'll like knowing that your mac and cheese contains a healthy dose.

4 TO 6 SERVINGS

1 (16-ounce) package pasta (any short chunky shape)

2 tablespoons vegan butter

4 cups cooked or thawed frozen cauliflower florets

½ cup unsweetened nondairy milk, plus more, as needed

1½ to 2 cups grated Cheddar-style, nondairy cheese

Salt, to taste

1. Cook the pasta according to the package directions until al dente, then drain and return to the pot. Toss with the vegan butter.

2. Meanwhile, combine the cauliflower, nondairy milk, and cheese in a blender. Blend until creamy and smooth, adding a bit more nondairy milk if needed.

3. Pour the sauce into the pot with the pasta and stir until completely combined. Return to medium-low heat for a few minutes, until everything is piping hot.

4. Season with salt and let stand for a few minutes (5 to 10 will do) to allow the pasta to absorb a bit of the sauce. Taste for salt, adjust, and serve.

COMPLETE THE MEAL
Serve with sautéed or steamed broccoli or green beans and **Mixed Greens with Chickpeas, Olives & Tomatoes** (page 49).

MUSHROOM PASTA PAPRIKASH

Garlic, mushrooms, and paprika pack plenty of flavor into this simple dish. You can use any short pasta shape for this, but I especially like it with shells or farfalle (bow ties).

4 TO 6 SERVINGS

10 to 12 ounces pasta (any short chunky shape)

2 tablespoons olive oil, preferably extra-virgin

3 to 4 cloves garlic

16 ounces pre-sliced mushrooms (see Note)

2 medium tomatoes, diced

2 to 3 teaspoons sweet or smoked paprika, or to taste

Salt and freshly ground pepper, to taste

1. Cook the pasta according to the package directions until al dente, then drain and return to the pot.

2. Heat the oil in a large skillet. Add the garlic and sauté over low heat until golden, 1 to 2 minutes. Add the mushrooms and cook until they're wilted and start to give off liquid, about 8 minutes. Add the tomatoes and continue to cook until they soften, about 3 to 4 minutes.

3. Combine the mushroom and tomato mixture with the cooked pasta in the pot. Stir in the paprika and season with salt and pepper. Cover and let stand for a few minutes to allow the pasta to absorb the flavors, then serve.

NOTE
Using pre-sliced mushrooms saves a fair amount of prep, especially in a recipe like this one that calls for a lot of them. First, make sure the mushrooms you buy look fresh. You'll want to give them a good rinsing in any case: Place them in a bowl with water to cover, give them a good swish around with your hands so any dirt will sink to the bottom, then scoop them up with your hands and transfer them to a colander. Rinse again.

MORE TIME / LESS LAZY
Of course, you can start with whole mushrooms. Stem, slice, and clean them, as usual.

COMPLETE THE MEAL
Cabbage & Apple Slaw (page 53) is a good partner for this dish. Add some green to the plate with steamed green beans.

HUNGARIAN-STYLE CABBAGE NOODLES

A classic Slavic-inspired dish is made simple by using bagged coleslaw cabbage. Of course, you can always use shredded fresh green cabbage if you prefer—about 6 cups is about what you'll need.

6 SERVINGS

2 tablespoons olive oil

1 large onion, quartered and thinly sliced

1 (16-ounce) bag coleslaw cabbage

10 to 12 ounces egg-free ribbon noodles (see Note)

1 tablespoon poppy seeds, more or less as desired

½ cup chopped fresh parsley

Salt and lots of freshly ground pepper, to taste

1. Heat the oil in a wide skillet or stir-fry pan. Add the onion and sauté over medium heat until golden.

2. Add the cabbage and about ¼ cup of water, then cover and cook over medium-high heat, stirring occasionally, until the cabbage is limp and just beginning to brown lightly, about 10 minutes.

3. Meanwhile, cook the noodles according to package directions until al dente.

4. Add the cabbage mixture and poppy seeds to the noodles and toss together gently.

5. Stir in the parsley and season to taste with salt and lots of pepper. Serve at once.

NOTE
Be aware that some ribbon noodles contain egg, so read labels and look for alternatives, like spelt ribbons or rombi. Or, if those aren't available, farfalle (bow-tie) pasta is nice in this dish as well.

COMPLETE THE MEAL
This is delicious with **Smoky Red Beans** (page 118) or even simpler, some sautéed vegan sausage. Complete with a salad of mixed greens, tomatoes, peppers, and carrots.

PEANUT SATAY NOODLES
WITH BROCCOLI OR CUCUMBER

Peanut noodles please almost everyone, even the pickiest of eaters (aka children). Using bottled Thai peanut satay sauce is quicker (and cheaper) than gathering up authentic ingredients like tamarind sauce, lemongrass, and red chile peppers. I use an organic store brand that's surprisingly low in calories for a sauce whose main ingredient is organic peanuts—only 100 calories and 4 grams of fat. There are many peanut satay brands available in the Asian foods section of your local grocery store. Most are vegan, but check the label just to be sure.

4 SERVINGS

8 to 10 ounces soba or udon noodles, or spaghetti

1 large broccoli crown, cut into small florets and pieces (or see variation using cucumber)

2 or 3 scallions, thinly sliced

1 cup bottled peanut satay sauce, or as needed

⅓ cup chopped peanuts or cashews

1. Cook the noodles according to the package directions. When the noodles are nearly done, plunge the broccoli into the simmering water and cook just until the broccoli turns bright green. This will take less than a minute. Drain the noodle and broccoli mixture well, then transfer to a serving bowl.

2. Add the scallions and peanut satay sauce and stir to combine with the noodles. Sprinkle the chopped nuts on top and serve at once.

OPTIONAL ADDITIONS

* Add a cup or two of another colorful vegetable, like grated carrots or red cabbage.

* Pass around sriracha or dried red pepper flakes to spice up individual servings.

VARIATIONS

* Cucumber can take the place of the broccoli. Use about half of a hothouse cucumber, quartered and thinly sliced, or 4 mini-cucumbers, thinly sliced. When draining the noodles and cucumber, rinse under cool running water until just warm. Drain well, then continue with the recipe.

* Use zucchini "noodles" in place of pasta. Keep them raw, or steam very lightly.

COMPLETE THE MEAL
Consider either **Corn & Edamame Salad** (page 67) or **Coconut Creamed Corn** (page 163) as accompaniments.

KASHA VARNITCHKES

It was a toss-up whether to include this recipe in the grains and beans chapter or this one, where it ultimately landed. Kasha Varnitchkes is a Jewish classic combining buckwheat groats and bowtie pasta (farfalle). This easy and comforting dish is a good introduction to an offbeat grain.

4 TO 6 SERVINGS

2 tablespoons olive oil

1 large or 2 medium onions, finely chopped

1 cup kasha (buckwheat groats)

1½ cups vegetable broth or 1½ cups water with 2 vegetable bouillon cubes

6 to 8 ounces cremini or white mushrooms, cleaned and sliced

8 ounces farfalle (bowtie pasta)

Salt and freshly ground pepper, to taste

1. Heat the oil in a stir-fry pan or large skillet. Add the onions and sauté over medium heat until golden. Add the kasha and stir to coat with the oil, then continue to sauté, stirring often, until the kasha is nicely toasted and the onions lightly browned here and there, about 7 minutes.

2. Stir in the broth and bring to a slow boil. Stir in the mushrooms, then lower the heat and simmer, uncovered, until the liquid is absorbed, about 15 minutes. Stir gently only once during this time to keep the kasha from getting mushy.

3. Meanwhile, cook the pasta according to the package directions until al dente, then drain.

4. When the kasha mixture is done, transfer it to a large serving bowl. Add the cooked pasta and toss together gently. Season with salt and pepper, and serve.

* If you are not a kasha fan, try this with bulgur (cracked wheat) instead: Combine 1 cup uncooked bulgur with 2 cups boiling water and 2 vegetable bouillon cubes in a heatproof bowl; let stand for 30 minutes, then stir to distribute the dissolved cubes. Or, to cook the grain more quickly, combine 1 cup uncooked bulgur with 2 cups broth or water with 2 bouillon cubes in a saucepan. Bring to a slow boil, then reduce the heat, cover, and simmer for about 15 minutes or until the water is absorbed.

OPTIONAL ADDITIONS

* Stir in chopped fresh dill and/or parsley, as desired.

COMPLETE THE MEAL

Serve with **Tahini, Carrot & Olive Salad** (page 60) and steamed broccoli or sautéed zucchini.

SOBA NOODLES WITH KALE OR COLLARDS

In this satisfying dish, soba noodles are laced through with lots of greens and flavored with a piquant dressing. It's a great way to get your loved ones to eat their greens!

4 SERVINGS

1 (8- to 10-ounce) bunch lacinato kale or collard greens

1 (8-ounce) package soba (buckwheat noodles)

4 scallions, white and green parts, thinly sliced

½ cup bottled sesame-ginger dressing, or as desired

Sriracha or dried hot red pepper flakes, to taste

Salt and freshly ground pepper, to taste

1. Cut the leaves of the greens away from their stems and rinse well. Stack 8 or so leaf halves on top of one another, then roll them up tightly from the narrow end. Cut into very narrow ribbons, then cut here and there in the other direction to shorten them.

2. Begin cooking the noodles according to the package directions. When the noodles are nearly tender, plunge the greens and the white parts of the scallions into the water with them. Continue to cook until the noodles are al dente and the greens are bright green and just done. Drain the noodle mixture and transfer to a serving bowl.

3. Stir in the dressing and green parts of the scallions, then season with sriracha or dried hot red pepper flakes. Add salt (be sparing, you may not need much, if any) and pepper to taste. Serve warm or at room temperature.

OPTIONAL ADDITION

* Black or white sesame seeds or hemp seeds for topping

COMPLETE THE MEAL

Serve with a platter of sliced baked tofu, tomatoes, and cucumbers. For fun, add vegetable spring rolls from your natural foods store or supermarket's freezer. For a more dressed-up meal, you might also consider adding **Hoisin-Glazed Eggplant** (page 165).

HOISIN-GINGER UDON NOODLES

There's something so toothsome—don't you love that word?—about thick udon noodles, but linguine works here, too. The udon noodles and hoisin sauce can usually be found in the Asian foods section of well-stocked supermarkets. This is a lovely dish to make when you're craving Asian flavors.

4 SERVINGS

1 (8-ounce) package udon noodles (or linguine)

6 to 8 stalks bok choy or 2 to 3 baby bok choy, thinly sliced

⅓ cup hoisin sauce, or to taste

1 tablespoon grated fresh or jarred ginger

¼ cup chopped cashews or peanuts, or 2 teaspoons sesame seeds

Salt and freshly ground pepper, to taste

1. Cook the noodles according to the package directions until al dente. Just before removing the noodles from the heat, plunge the bok choy into the water, then drain the mixture and transfer to a serving bowl.

2. Combine the noodles and bok choy with the remaining ingredients and toss together. Serve at once.

OPTIONAL ADDITIONS

* Per my usual suggestion, pass around sriracha sauce for anyone who'd like to spice up their noodles.

* Garnish with thinly sliced scallions.

VARIATION

* Use a small head of romaine lettuce, thinly sliced, in place of bok choy.

COMPLETE THE MEAL
Serve with **Sweet & Savory Sautéed Tofu** (page 83) or **Orange-Glazed Tofu** (page 82) and a steamed or sautéed green veggie of your choice. Or, you could do these accompaniments a bit in reverse—make **Spicy Sesame Broccoli** (page 167) and a platter of sliced baked tofu, unembellished.

STREAMLINED VEGETABLE LO MEIN

Versions of vegetable lo mein have made their way into a few of my cookbooks since it's something I crave regularly. This recipe, the easiest variation yet, gets its veggie goodness from bagged coleslaw. It makes a heaping helping with 6 generous servings or more, and is lighter on oil than the take-out variety.

6 OR MORE SERVINGS

12 ounces thin or regular spaghetti

1 tablespoon safflower or other neutral oil

4 to 5 scallions, white and green parts, sliced

1 (16-ounce) bag coleslaw (preferably with carrots)

½ to ¾ cup bottled sesame teriyaki marinade, or as needed

Freshly ground pepper, to taste

1. Cook the noodles according to the package directions until al dente, then drain.

2. Meanwhile, heat the oil in a stir-fry pan or large skillet. Add the white parts of the scallions and sauté over medium heat for a minute or two. Add the coleslaw and stir-fry over medium-high heat for 4 to 5 minutes, or until the vegetables are just tender-crisp. Add a small amount of water to keep the pan moist, if needed.

3. Add the cooked noodles to the pan and toss together with the cabbage. Stir in the teriyaki marinade and season with pepper. Serve at once.

OPTIONAL ADDITIONS
When the mood strikes, any one or two of these optional ingredients are welcome. Add any of the first five to the pan at the same time as the cabbage, and the last three at the end.)

* Sliced mushrooms (about 8 ounces)

* Baby corn (15-ounce can, drained)

* Very small broccoli florets (about 2 cups)

* Snow peas (a big handful or two, trimmed)

* Slender green beans (about 4 ounces)

* Sesame oil (1 to 2 teaspoons)

* Grated fresh or jarred ginger (2 to 3 teaspoons)

* Dried hot red pepper flakes, to taste

COMPLETE THE MEAL
This goes nicely with **Lazy General Tso's Tofu** (page 85) or **Corn & Edamame Salad** (page 67).

EASIEST VEGAN PARMESAN-STYLE TOPPING

Most recipes for homemade vegan Parmesan are a basic combination of nutritional yeast plus ground cashews or almonds. This version is even easier because no machine is required. Just two key ingredients—almond flour (found in most natural foods stores) and "nooch"—make a nutritious topping for pasta (and anything else you'd like to sprinkle it on). A tablespoon or two provides you with a good dose of vitamin B_{12} from the nutritional yeast, while the almond flour is a great source of vitamin E and calcium. This super-tasty topping tastes amazing on many of the pasta dishes in this chapter.

MAKES 1 CUP

½ **cup nutritional yeast**

½ **cup almond flour**

¼ **teaspoon salt, or to taste**

1. Combine all the ingredients in a small bowl and mix together thoroughly.

NOTE
Store any unused portion in an airtight container in the refrigerator, where it will keep for many weeks.

6

GRAINS & BEANS

rains and beans are the **WORKHORSES OF THE PLANT-BASED DIET.** True and loyal friends in the kitchen, they've been paired together throughout the ages in the major cuisines of the world. And I'll bet they'll outlast and surpass any trendy food that comes along. Give me beans over meat imitators any day! Once considered starchy, even fattening, beans (aka legumes), the "poor man's food," have earned respect as an **EXCELLENT SOURCE OF COMPLEX CARBOHYDRATES, FIBER, AND PROTEIN.** Like beans, grains provide these building blocks of a healthful diet, as well.

Although it is a bit of a cliché to combine grains and beans in a single chapter, I decided to do so, not because of the old notion that you must combine them in the same meal for complete protein, but because they simply go together so well. **VERSATILE, SATISFYING, AND INEXPENSIVE,** they deserve a prominent place in your repertoire.

SALSA BLACK BEANS

This hearty dish of black beans and salsa has long been one of my favorite emergency dinners, and perhaps it will become one of yours, too. Served with the suggested menu options following the recipe, it's part of a fun weeknight fiesta.

4 TO 6 SERVINGS

1 tablespoon olive oil

4 to 6 cloves garlic, minced

2 (15-ounce) cans black beans, drained and rinsed

Juice of ½ to 1 lime, to taste (plus another lime for garnish, if desired)

1 (16-ounce) jar salsa (your favorite variety, see Note)

¼ cup minced fresh cilantro, plus more for topping

1. Heat the oil in a large saucepan. Add the garlic and sauté over low heat until golden, 1 to 2 minutes. Add the beans, lime juice, and ½ cup water and cook over medium heat until the mixture comes to a gentle simmer.

2. Mash some of the beans in the skillet with a potato masher until a nice thick base forms. Add the salsa and simmer gently for 5 minutes longer. Stir in the cilantro, and serve.

3. Pass around extra cilantro for topping individual portions, and if you'd like, a lime wedge or two.

COMPLETE THE MEAL
Serve with or over hot cooked rice or quinoa. Add an easy slaw, like **Corn Slaw** (page 56). **Cinnamon Sautéed Bananas** (page 207) give this meal an unexpected twist as a side dish. Pass around some tortilla chips if you'd like. Or, pair with **Avocado and Sweet Potato Quesadillas or Soft Tacos** (page 184) or **Spinach & Bell Pepper Quesadillas** (page 186).

NOTE
Use an interesting variety of salsa, such as chipotle or pineapple.

POLENTA WITH BLACK BEANS & SPINACH

Using prepared polenta is a nifty way to add variety to the dinner repertoire. One of my long-time favorites, this recipe for pan-grilled polenta is topped with a colorful combination of black beans, roasted red pepper, and spinach. As a main dish, it's light and satisfying. It can also be served as a hearty, warm appetizer.

3 TO 4 SERVINGS

1 (18-ounce) tube polenta

1 tablespoon olive oil

2 to 3 cloves garlic, minced

1 (15- to 16-ounce) can black beans, drained and rinsed

1 roasted red pepper (from a jar or the supermarket olive bar), drained and cut into short strips

4 to 5 ounces baby spinach, rinsed

Salt and freshly ground pepper, to taste

1. Cut the polenta into 12 even slices, each about ½ inch thick.

2. Use a little of the olive oil to lightly coat a wide nonstick skillet or griddle. Arrange the polenta slices in the skillet and cook over medium-high heat until golden and crisp, about 8 minutes per side.

3. Meanwhile, heat the remaining olive oil in a medium skillet or stir-fry pan. Add the garlic and sauté over low heat for a minute or so, just until golden.

4. Add the beans and roasted pepper, stir together, and cook over medium heat until well heated through. Add the spinach, cover, and cook until it just wilts, 1 to 2 minutes. Stir the mixture together, season with salt (you may not need much, if any) and pepper, and remove from the heat.

5. To serve, arrange 3 or 4 polenta slices on each plate and spoon the bean mixture evenly over each serving.

COMPLETE THE MEAL
Serve with a green salad using whatever you've got on hand, or choose from the **Mixed Greens Salads** on pages 44 to 49. For a bigger meal, add some baked or microwaved potatoes or sweet potatoes.

SMOKY RED BEANS

While visiting New Orleans some years ago, I came across a tiny vegetarian eatery, since closed, that served meatless versions of local fare. One of the most iconic of Creole dishes is red beans and rice. It sounds like it would be safe for vegans, but the traditional version contains meaty things. The owner-chef's secret ingredient was peanut butter, which boosts the smoky flavor of the seasonings. This simple recipe for red beans borrows from that inspiration. While it might not be the prettiest dish, the flavor is sublime!

4 TO 6 SERVINGS

1 tablespoon olive oil

3 to 4 cloves garlic, minced

2 (15-ounce) cans small red beans, drained and rinsed

2 to 3 teaspoons barbecue seasoning, to taste

2 tablespoons smooth peanut butter

Juice of ½ to 1 lemon or lime (about 2 tablespoons), or to taste

1. Heat the oil in a large saucepan. Add the garlic and sauté over low heat until golden, 1 to 2 minutes. Add the beans and ½ cup water. Cook over medium heat until the mixture comes to a gentle simmer.

2. Mash some of the beans in the skillet with a potato masher until there's a nice thick base. Add the remaining ingredients and simmer gently for 5 minutes longer. Serve at once in shallow bowls.

OPTIONAL ADDITIONS
Add one of the following to the finished dish:

* About ¼ cup minced fresh cilantro or parsley

* A couple of teaspoons of fresh thyme or oregano

COMPLETE THE MEAL
This can be served side by side with or over cooked brown rice (go an easy step further with Spinach & Dill Rice, page 135) or another grain. If you skip the grain, you can scoop up this tasty bean dish with fresh flour tortillas. For a delicious salad accompaniment, choose Happy Trails Kale & Apple Salad (page 59) or Kale & Avocado Salad (page 58).

SKILLET BBQ BEANS & GREENS

Beans and greens simply belong together, and a double dose of barbecue flavors makes them shine. Your favorite ready-made barbecue sauce gets an extra pop of flavor from barbecue seasoning blend. Look for barbecue seasonings in your supermarket's spice section.

**4 SERVINGS AS A MAIN DISH;
6 OR MORE SERVINGS AS A SIDE DISH**

6 to 8 collard green or lacinato kale leaves

1 tablespoon olive oil

2 to 3 cloves garlic, finely chopped

2 (15- to 16-ounce) cans pinto, pink, or cannellini beans, drained and rinsed

½ cup barbecue sauce (your favorite variety), plus more, as needed

2 teaspoons barbecue seasoning (mesquite, smoky maple, etc.), or more, to taste

1. Cut the collard or lacinato leaves away from the stems. Stack 4 to 6 similar-size leaf halves on top of one another. Roll up tightly from one of the narrow ends, then slice into very thin ribbons. Chop the ribbons in a few places to shorten them. Repeat as needed.

2. Heat the oil in a medium skillet or stir-fry pan with a couple of tablespoons of water. Add the garlic and greens and cook over medium-high heat, stirring often, until the greens are bright and tender-crisp, about 4 to 5 minutes.

3. Stir in the beans, barbecue sauce, and seasoning and continue to cook about 3 to 5 minutes longer, until the beans are hot and nicely glazed. Taste to see if you'd like to add more sauce or seasoning, then serve.

COMPLETE THE MEAL
I like to accompany BBQ-flavored dishes with coleslaw as a nice flavor contrast; for this one, I'd recommend Cabbage & Apple Slaw (page 53) or Pineapple Coleslaw (page 54). To bulk up the meal, you can add a hot cooked grain or baked or microwaved sweet potato.

GARLIC-HERB BEANS OR LENTILS

This is a basic preparation I use often for all kinds of legumes, and it can be served as a main dish or, in smaller portions, as a side dish for meals that need a protein boost. Although I usually use chickpeas or pinto beans, any variety of legumes, including brown lentils, will work.

I'm always looking for ways to use fresh watercress, one of the most nutrient-dense foods on the planet, and this is just the place to use it as a change of pace from the usual leafy herbs.

**4 SERVINGS AS A MAIN DISH;
6 SERVINGS OR MORE AS A SIDE DISH**

1 tablespoon olive oil

3 to 4 cloves garlic, minced

2 (15- to 16-ounce) cans beans or lentils (see Notes), drained and rinsed

Juice of ½ to 1 whole lemon or lime, to taste

2 scallions, thinly sliced

Salt and freshly ground pepper, to taste

¼ cup to ½ cup finely chopped fresh parsley or cilantro, or about half a bunch of chopped watercress leaves and stems

1. Heat the oil in a skillet. Add the garlic and sauté over low heat until golden, about 1 to 2 minutes.

2. Add the beans and ½ cup water and bring to a simmer.

3. Mash enough of the beans in the skillet with a potato masher or large fork to make a nice thick base. Add lemon juice, tasting as you add. Stir in the scallions and season with salt and pepper. (If using canned beans, you may not need additional salt, though organic beans are usually less salty.)

4. Stir in a small amount of chopped parsley or cilantro, or pass it around for topping individual portions. Serve on its own or over grains or pasta.

NOTES
Use any kind of legumes, choosing from red, pink, pinto, black, or white beans; chickpeas; or brown lentils. You can also combine two different kinds.

If you're using organic canned beans, whose liquid is less salty and viscous, reserve ½ cup of the liquid to use in place of water.

COMPLETE THE MEAL
See the menus suggested with **Spinach Pesto Pasta** (page 99) and **Chile Cheese Grits** (page 125), both of which include this recipe.

EASIEST CHILI BEAN TOSTADAS

Crisp tortillas piled with layers of tasty toppings are practically a one-dish meal, with protein, carbs, and salad in one neat (or to be honest, a little messy) package. And you can make this easy dinner dish super-easy by using ready-made chili and salsa. For the chili, I use Amy's® brand, but any natural vegan variety will do.

4 SERVINGS

8 good-quality corn tortillas

2 (15-ounce) cans chili (any vegan variety)

1 medium ripe avocado

Shredded lettuce, as needed

Salsa (your favorite variety; see suggestions above), as needed

OPTIONAL ADDITIONS

* Vegan cheese shreds, any flavor (add as a layer over the chili)

* 2 limes, quartered, to squeeze onto the tostadas

COMPLETE THE MEAL

Serve with fresh corn on the cob or baked or microwaved sweet potatoes. **Super-Easy Guacamole** (page 22; or store-bought) and tortilla chips wouldn't hurt, either!

TO TOAST THE TORTILLAS IN THE OVEN:

1. Preheat the oven to 375°F. Place the tortillas on a baking sheet. Bake for 10 minutes, or until crisp and dry, and just starting to be touched with golden-brown spots.

TO TOAST THE TORTILLAS ON THE STOVETOP:

1. Heat a large skillet over medium-high heat, then toast the tortillas (two or three at a time, depending on the size of the skillet) for about 5 minutes or so on each side, until crisp and touched with golden-brown spots.

2. Meanwhile, heat the chili in a saucepan until piping hot, then transfer to a bowl for serving.

3. Peel and dice the avocado. Place in a small bowl. Place the lettuce and salsa in separate small bowls.

4. Let everyone assemble their tostadas as follows: a layer of shredded lettuce, followed by the chili, salsa, and avocado. Eat out of hand with plenty of napkins!

SALSA VERDE BEAN BURRITOS

Salsa verde, made from tomatillos, gives these burritos a nice tang. Since this type of salsa's flavor is right between mild and hot, you can push these burritos in a milder or spicier direction, depending on your choice of refried beans and vegan cheese, since both are available in varying degrees of heat.

MAKES 6 BURRITOS (3 TO 6 SERVINGS)

1 (15-ounce) can vegan refried beans (try spicy, green chile, etc.)

1 (15- to 16-ounce) can pinto or pink beans, drained and rinsed

1 cup salsa verde (tomatillo salsa)

1 cup vegan cheese shreds (try pepper jack)

6 burrito-size (10- to 12-inch) soft flour tortillas, at room temperature

1. Combine the refried beans, pinto beans, and salsa verde in a saucepan. Bring to a simmer, then turn off the heat and stir in the cheese.

2. For each burrito, scoop about ¾ cup of the filling into the center of each tortilla. Fold two ends in over the filling, then roll up. Cut in half to serve or keep whole, as desired.

COMPLETE THE MEAL
Serve with **Mixed Greens with Tomato, Corn & Avocado** (page 45), **Kale & Avocado Salad** (page 58), or any simple green salad. **Super-Easy Guacamole** (page 22; or store-bought) and tortilla chips are welcome, but entirely optional.

CHICKPEA MASALA

I've always been too lazy to roast, grind, mix, and measure the myriad spices that create the complex flavors of Indian cuisine. Now, if you crave Indian flavors, you have an option other than going out to eat or buying take-out—just grab a jar of Indian simmer sauce. This dish takes only about ten minutes to make, even if you move at a glacial pace.

3 TO 4 SERVINGS

2 (15-ounce) cans chickpeas, drained and rinsed

1 large or two medium tomatoes, diced

1 (12-ounce) jar or container Indian simmer sauce of your choice (see Note)

4 to 5 ounces baby spinach, rinsed

¼ to ½ cup fresh cilantro, chopped

1. Combine the chickpeas, tomato, and Indian simmer sauce in a pan and bring to a simmer. Add the spinach, cover, and cook until it wilts down. Stir the spinach into the mixture.

2. Stir in the cilantro and serve.

NOTE
For this dish, I usually choose Madras curry, which is fairly spicy. You can use any other vegan variety of this kind of sauce. Goan coconut, tikka masala, and jalfrezi are usually vegan, but check the labels to make sure.

COMPLETE THE MEAL
This is nice with a simple carrot-raisin salad: Combine some grated carrots and raisins (no need for precise amounts) in a serving bowl. Add enough lemon juice to provide a little tang. Add a fresh flatbread, or feel free to add a hot cooked grain if you'd like a heftier meal. Whole-grain couscous works well and fits with the minutes-to-the-table pace of the meal.

LENTILS & KIDNEY BEANS JALFREZI

Inspired by a traditional Indian recipe that combines two tasty, high-protein legumes and incorporates 15 to 20 ingredients, many of which are spices, here is my take on a drastically simplified version. The secret to this nearly-instant preparation is a jar of Indian jalfrezi sauce. I like to go with this medium-spicy sauce, but use any vegan variety of Indian simmer sauce you prefer. See more about these sauces on page xv.

4 SERVINGS

1 (15-ounce) can brown lentils, drained and rinsed

1 (15-ounce) can kidney beans, drained and rinsed

2 to 3 scallions, sliced

1 (12- to 16-ounce) jar Indian jalfrezi sauce (or other Indian simmer sauce of your choice)

Cilantro, as desired (save some for garnish)

1. Combine all the ingredients in a saucepan and bring to a simmer. Cook gently for 5 to 7 minutes, until piping hot.

COMPLETE THE MEAL
Serve with hot cooked rice, couscous, or quinoa. Add a colorful salad using lettuce or mixed greens, peppers, carrots, tomatoes, and cucumbers, and your favorite dressing.

CHILE CHEESE GRITS

A tasty and speedy dish, this is a longtime favorite that my family has always loved. Paired with a bean dish, this makes a hearty meal.

4 TO 6 SERVINGS

1 cup stone-ground grits

1½ to 2 cups cooked fresh or thawed frozen corn kernels

1 to 2 jalapeño peppers, seeded and finely chopped

1½ tablespoons vegan butter

1 cup cheddar-style vegan cheese

Salt to taste

1. Bring 4 cups of water to a slow boil in a large saucepan. Remove the saucepan from the heat and turn the heat down to low. Slowly whisk in the grits, whisking constantly to avoid lumps. Cover and cook gently over low heat, whisking occasionally, for 15 to 20 minutes, or until tender and thick. (Or follow the package instructions, as they vary from one brand to another.)

2. Stir in the remaining ingredients, except the salt, and cook for 2 to 3 minutes longer, until the cheese is well melted.

3. Season with salt and serve at once in bowls.

OPTIONAL ADDITION

✴ During the summer, I like to add a diced tomato or two. Add them along with the corn and other ingredients.

COMPLETE THE MEAL

Garlic-Herb Beans or Lentils (page 120) using black or pinto beans makes a perfect companion to this dish. Add a simple green salad or Slaw (pages 52 to 57) to round out the meal.

GRITS OR POLENTA WITH GREENS
& CARAMELIZED ONION

The combination of mellow grits or polenta, sweet onion, and tender greens practically melts in your mouth. There's not much difference between grits and polenta in terms of flavor, but grits are usually a bit coarser in texture. In any case, both grits and polenta should be considered more often as a grain option.

4 TO 6 SERVINGS

1 cup stone-ground corn grits or coarse cornmeal (see Note)

2 tablespoons vegan butter

1½ tablespoons olive oil

1 large red or yellow onion, quartered and thinly sliced

2 to 3 cloves garlic, minced

8 ounces fresh greens (chard, kale, or collards), or 5 to 6 ounces baby spinach, rinsed

Salt and freshly ground pepper, to taste

1. Bring 4 cups of water to a slow boil in a large saucepan. Remove the saucepan from the heat and turn the heat down to low. Slowly whisk in the grits, whisking constantly to avoid lumps. Return the saucepan to the heat, cover, and cook the grits gently over low heat, whisking occasionally, for 15 to 20 minutes, or until tender and thick. (Or follow the package instructions, as they vary from one brand to another.) Remove the saucepan from the heat. Stir in the vegan butter and season with salt. Set the grits aside.

2. Heat about half of the oil in a wide skillet or stir-fry pan. Add the onions and sauté over low heat until golden. Add the garlic and continue to sauté until the onions are soft and lightly browned. Remove this mixture from the pan and set aside.

3. While the onion and garlic mixture is cooking, rinse the greens you'll be using. Unless you're using spinach, strip leaves away from the stems. Cut the leaves into ribbons or bite-size pieces. If using kale or chard, slice the stems thinly and use them as well. If using collards, discard the stems. If using baby spinach, you needn't do any stemming or chopping at all.

4. Heat the remaining oil in a large pan. Add the greens and just enough water to keep the bottom of the pan moist. Sprinkle in a little salt, which will help retain their color. Cover and cook the greens until tender, but let them stay nice and bright. Press down on the greens to extract any excess liquid, then drain from the pan.

5. To serve, divide the grits or polenta among 4 to 6 individual bowls, depending on how many you're serving. Top each with the greens, then the onion mixture. Serve at once.

NOTE

Coarse cornmeal, otherwise known as polenta (and not the same thing as the kind of prepared polenta that comes in tubes) is similar to grits. Bob's Red Mill® markets its grits interchangeably with polenta, though that's not always the case.

OPTIONAL ADDITIONS

＊ This is delicious topped with a scattering of sliced sun-dried tomatoes or chopped briny olives.

＊ Add a cup or two of cooked fresh or thawed frozen corn kernels to the grits once they're cooked.

COMPLETE THE MEAL

For a delectable pairing, serve this with **Sweet & Smoky Tempeh Strips** (page 92) or a store-bought equivalent like Fakin' Bacon®. Add a platter of sliced tomatoes and colorful bell pepper.

QUINOA WITH
CAULIFLOWER & CRANBERRIES

With just a few ingredients, this dish showcases sweet, savory, and nutty flavors. In larger servings, it can be a main dish; in smaller portions, it's wonderful as a side-by-side dish with roasted vegetable and chickpea dishes.

4 TO 6 SERVINGS

1½ cups quinoa, rinsed in a fine sieve

1 small head cauliflower, cut into small pieces and florets

1½ tablespoons olive oil

3 to 4 scallions, thinly sliced, green and white parts separate

½ cup dried cranberries or raisins

½ cup crushed walnuts or toasted cashews

Salt and freshly ground pepper, to taste

1. Combine the quinoa with 3 cups of water in a large saucepan. Bring to a slow boil, then turn down the heat, cover, and simmer until the water is absorbed, about 15 minutes. If the quinoa isn't done to your liking, add another ½ cup of water and cook until absorbed.

2. Meanwhile, combine the cauliflower with about ½ cup water in a stir-fry pan. Cover and cook for 5 to 7 minutes over medium heat, or until the cauliflower is tender-crisp. Drizzle in the olive oil, then add the white parts of the scallion. Turn the heat up to medium-high and cook, stirring often, until the cauliflower starts to get golden-brown spots here and there.

3. When the quinoa is done, add it to the cauliflower mixture, along with the cranberries and green parts of the scallions.

4. Add the walnuts, toss everything together, and season with salt and pepper. Serve at once.

LESS TIME / EVEN LAZIER
Substitute a 16-ounce bag of frozen cauliflower florets (thawed) for the fresh.

COMPLETE THE MEAL
Pair with **Mixed Greens with Beets & Bell Pepper** (page 48). For a heftier meal, add **Smoky Red Beans** (page 118). For a festive meal worthy of the winter holidays, accompany with **Sweet & Savory Roasted Butternut Squash** (page 150) and **Kale & Cabbage Slaw** (page 55).

QUINOA WITH TENDER GREENS & ARTICHOKE HEARTS

Another tasty quinoa dish, this one is dressed up with marinated artichokes that add flavor and eye appeal. Feel free to experiment with the varieties of tender greens—baby spinach, baby arugula, or baby kale. They all usually can be found side by side at the farmers' market or supermarket.

4 TO 6 SERVINGS

1½ cups quinoa, rinsed in a fine sieve

2 teaspoons salt-free seasoning blend or 2 vegetable bouillon cubes

1 tablespoon olive oil

2 to 3 cloves garlic, minced

4 to 6 ounces baby spinach, baby arugula, or baby kale, rinsed

1 to 1½ cups marinated artichoke hearts, quartered (see Note)

Salt and freshly ground pepper, to taste

1. Combine the quinoa with 3 cups of water and the seasoning blend or bouillon cubes in a large saucepan. Bring to a slow boil, then turn down the heat, cover, and simmer until the water is absorbed, about 15 minutes. If the quinoa isn't done to your liking, add another ½ cup of water and cook until absorbed.

2. Heat the oil in a wide skillet or stir-fry pan. Add the garlic and sauté for a minute or two, until golden. Add the greens to the skillet, cover, and cook until just barely wilted.

3. When the quinoa is done, add it to the skillet along with the artichoke hearts (reserve liquid). Stir together. Drizzle in just enough liquid from the artichoke hearts to add moisture and flavor.

4. Season with salt and pepper, and serve.

NOTE

You can use an 8- to 12-ounce jar of marinated artichoke hearts, or purchase them by weight from your supermarket's olive bar.

OPTIONAL ADDITION

✳ Add a sprinkling of dried hot red pepper flakes for a touch of heat.

COMPLETE THE MEAL

Round this meal out simply with **Two-Bean Salad** (page 66) and a platter of sliced tomatoes, cucumbers, and bell peppers.

SALSA VERDE QUINOA

Salsa verde (tomatillo salsa), with its somewhat smoky flavor, makes a bold statement in this quinoa skillet preparation. Any leftovers can be used as a dip with tortilla chips or to make Super-Easy Guacamole (page 22).

4 TO 6 SERVINGS

1½ cups quinoa (any color), rinsed in a fine sieve

1 cup salsa verde (tomatillo salsa), or more, to taste

3 to 4 scallions, thinly sliced

1 cup shredded vegan cheddar (pre-shredded, or grated from a block)

¼ to ½ cup chopped fresh cilantro or parsley

Salt and freshly ground pepper, to taste

1. Combine the quinoa with 3 cups of water in a stir-fry pan or deep skillet. Bring to a slow boil, then turn down the heat, cover, and simmer until the water is absorbed, about 15 minutes. If the quinoa isn't done to your liking, add another ½ cup of water and cook until absorbed.

2. Stir in the salsa, scallions, and cheddar. Cook for 10 minutes, stirring occasionally until the mixture gets nice and toasty.

3. Stir in the cilantro, season with salt and pepper, and serve.

COMPLETE THE MEAL
For a light yet luscious meal, serve with steamed or roasted asparagus, sliced avocado, and sliced beets (freshly cooked, pickled, or prepared packaged beets like Love™ Beets). For a heftier meal, add Two-Bean Salad (page 66).

CHEESY QUINOA & BROCCOLI SKILLET

This easy, cheesy skillet dish is pure comfort. It makes a generous amount, so you might enjoy taking some to work the next day or coming home to leftovers.

6 SERVINGS

1½ cups quinoa, rinsed in a fine sieve

1 tablespoon olive oil

1 large onion, chopped

2 medium broccoli crowns, cut into bite-size pieces

2 medium tomatoes, diced, or 15-ounce can diced tomatoes, lightly drained

1½ cups shredded vegan cheddar cheese

Salt and freshly ground pepper, to taste

1. Combine the quinoa with 3 cups of water in a large saucepan. Bring to a slow boil, then turn down the heat, cover, and simmer until the water is absorbed, about 15 minutes. If the quinoa isn't done to your liking, add another ½ cup of water and cook until absorbed.

2. Meanwhile, heat the oil in a large skillet or stir-fry pan. Add the onion and sauté until golden.

3. Add the broccoli and about ¼ cup of water. Cover and steam until the broccoli is just a little beyond tender-crisp, but still bright green, about 5 to 7 minutes.

4. When the quinoa is done, add it to the broccoli along with the tomatoes and cheese. Cook the mixture, stirring often, for 5 to 7 minutes longer, or until the cheese is nicely melted and everything is piping hot. Serve at once.

LESS TIME / EVEN LAZIER
Use a 16-ounce bag frozen broccoli florets in place of the fresh broccoli. It's not as good that way, but it will do in a pinch—or when you don't feel like chopping.

COMPLETE THE MEAL
Choose one of the fruity slaws—**Cabbage & Apple Slaw** (page 53) or **Pineapple Coleslaw** (page 54)—for a delightful flavor contrast.

COUSCOUS CURRY
WITH PEAS & CASHEWS

This couscous has it all—it's colorful, with bright green peas and dried fruit, nicely textured with nuts, and flavored with the complex Indian simmer sauce that I've made much use of in this book. And, it's ready in minutes, leaving plenty of time to build a meal around it.

4 TO 6 SERVINGS

1½ cups couscous, preferably whole grain

1 cup frozen green peas, completely thawed

½ cup raisins, dried cherries, or dried cranberries

1 cup Indian simmer sauce of your choice (see more on page xv)

½ cup chopped cashews

Salt and freshly ground pepper, to taste

1. Combine the couscous with 3 cups of water in a wide skillet or stir-fry pan. Bring to a simmer, then cover and let stand off the heat for 5 to 10 minutes, or until the water is absorbed.

2. Add the remaining ingredients, stir together well, then cook, stirring often, for 2 to 3 minutes longer. Serve at once.

VARIATION

* Substitute the same amount of quinoa for the couscous, and cook according to quinoa instructions.

COMPLETE THE MEAL

Serve with **Lemon-Pepper Tofu Cutlets with Tartar Sauce** (page 84) or **Garlic-Herb Beans or Lentils** (page 120) and a simple green salad.

ALMOND BASMATI RICE PILAF

This simple rice pilaf recipe highlights aromatic brown basmati rice. As a side dish, it enhances many kinds of meals and is especially good with curries and bean dishes.

6 SERVINGS

1 (32-ounce) carton low-sodium vegetable broth

1½ cups brown basmati rice, rinsed

½ to ⅔ cup sliced or slivered toasted almonds

½ cup dark or golden raisins

¼ to ½ cup finely chopped fresh cilantro or parsley

Salt and freshly ground pepper, to taste

1. Combine the broth and rice in a medium saucepan and bring to a slow boil. Reduce the heat and simmer gently until the broth is absorbed, about 30 minutes.

2. Stir the remaining ingredients into the rice and serve.

VARIATION
* Replace ½ cup of the brown basmati rice with forbidden black rice or wild rice.

OPTIONAL ADDITIONS
* Stir as much chopped fresh cilantro as you'd like into the finished pilaf.
* Stir a tablespoon or two of vegan buttery spread or fragrant nut oil into the finished pilaf.

COMPLETE THE MEAL
For a hearty meal, pair with **Lentils & Kidney Beans Jalfrezi** (page 124). Add a platter of raw vegetables—cherry tomatoes, baby carrots, and sliced cucumbers.

SPINACH & DILL RICE

Here's a brown rice dish that incorporates lots of fresh spinach and the fresh flavor of dill. Why serve plain brown rice when it's so easy to add a few embellishments?

4 TO 6 SERVINGS

- 1 cup raw long-grain brown rice, rinsed
- 4 to 6 ounces baby spinach
- 2 to 3 scallions, thinly sliced
- ¼ cup chopped fresh dill
- Juice of ½ to 1 lemon, to taste
- Salt and freshly ground pepper, to taste

1. Combine the rice with 2½ cups of water in a deep skillet or stir-fry pan. Bring to a slow boil, then lower the heat, cover, and simmer gently until the water is absorbed, about 30 to 35 minutes. If the rice isn't done to your liking, add another ½ cup of water and simmer until absorbed.

2. When the rice is done, add the spinach in batches, stirring it in as it wilts down. Stir the remaining ingredients into the rice and serve at once.

OPTIONAL ADDITION
* Add a tablespoon or two of extra-virgin olive oil for a richer flavor.

COMPLETE THE MEAL
Serve with Smoky Red Beans (page 118) and add a simple green salad. Or, pair with Pinto Bean & Avocado Salad (page 68).

ITALIAN-STYLE
RICE & PEAS

Inspired by the Italian classic *risi e bisi*, this comforting dish of rice and green peas gets a flavor boost from sun-dried tomatoes.

6 SERVINGS

1½ tablespoons olive oil, preferably extra-virgin

1 large onion, finely chopped

1 cup raw long-grain brown rice, rinsed

2½ cups vegetable broth or water with 2 vegetable bouillon cubes

2 cups frozen green peas, thawed

½ cup thinly sliced sun-dried tomatoes (see Note)

Salt and freshly ground pepper, to taste

NOTE

This is best with oil-packed sun-dried tomatoes, but use oil-free if you prefer. Just make sure they're nice and moist. If need be, rehydrate briefly in a small amount of hot water.

OPTIONAL ADDITION

* Garnish the dish with sliced basil leaves or finely chopped parsley—as much as you'd like.

COMPLETE THE MEAL

This is delicious with **Tahini-Lemon Greens** (page 162) or **Sweet & Savory Roasted Butternut Squash** (page 150) and a simple **Carrot-Raisin Salad** (see easy instructions under **Chickpea Masala**, page 123).

1. Heat the oil in a large saucepan. Add the onion and sauté over medium heat until golden.

2. Combine rice and broth in a medium saucepan and bring to a slow boil. Reduce the heat and simmer gently with the cover ajar until the broth is absorbed, about 30 minutes. If the rice isn't done to your liking, add ½ cup more broth (or water) and cook until absorbed.

3. Stir in the peas and cook just until heated through. Stir in the dried tomatoes. Season with salt and pepper, and serve at once.

FARRO WITH MUSHROOMS & CARROTS

Rounding out this chapter is a dish that gives you a taste of farro. This hearty grain is an ancient wheat, long beloved in Italian cuisine. Filled with fiber and high in iron, it can be swapped in for rice and barley in all kinds of dishes. Quick-cooking farro is usually found in the pasta aisle of well-stocked supermarkets, shelved with other Italian products. It's already nicely seasoned, so you can focus on adding plenty of vegetables to boost the modest quantity of grain.

4 TO 6 SERVINGS

1 (7- to 8-ounce) package quick-cooking farro

1½ tablespoons olive oil

1 large onion, quartered and thinly sliced

2 cups grated carrots (use pre-grated if you'd like)

8 to 10 ounces cremini mushrooms, cleaned, stemmed, and sliced

¼ cup chopped fresh dill or parsley

Salt and freshly ground pepper, to taste

1. Cook the farro according to the package directions.

2. Meanwhile, heat the oil in a large skillet or stir-fry pan. Add the onion and sauté over medium-low heat until translucent. Add the carrots and continue to sauté until both vegetables are golden brown.

3. Add the mushrooms to the skillet. Cover and cook over medium heat until wilted, about 5 minutes. Drizzle a little water into the skillet if needed to keep the skillet moist.

4. When the farro is done, add it to the skillet along with the dill. Season with salt (taste first; you may not need much) and pepper, and serve.

VARIATION

* Though farro is a type of wheat, it's quite comparable to barley. Feel free to swap quick-cooking barley for the farro.

COMPLETE THE MEAL
Pair with **Two-Bean Salad** (page 66) and some red or yellow cherry tomatoes for a lovely meal.

7

VEGETABLES FRONT & CENTER

f grains, beans, tofu, and tempeh are the building blocks of a healthful and satisfying diet, fresh **VEGETABLES ARE THE MORTAR**, providing valuable vitamins and antioxidants and making the plant-based plate truly crave-worthy. Vegetables, like beans, have been **RISING STARS** of the food world of late, no longer occupying the most boring little corner of the plate.

This chapter presents an array of quick and easy recipes that **MAKE VEGGIES APPEALING**. Let's toss out that old cliché that has a proverbial Mom admonishing a reluctant eater to "eat your vegetables." Eating vegetables shouldn't be seen as something to get over with, or as a promise for dessert. This chapter is here to **ENCOURAGE YOU TO INDULGE** in even more of a good thing. The recipes that follow are suggested in menus or pairings scattered through the other chapters. Feel free to serve them in other combinations.

CURRIED GREENS SMASHED POTATOES

Greens enveloped in a luscious Indian simmer sauce couldn't be a tastier topping for smashed potatoes.

4 SERVINGS

4 medium-large golden potatoes

1 (5- to 6-ounce) package mixed power greens (see Note) or baby spinach

2 scallions, sliced

¼ cup chopped fresh cilantro

1 cup Indian simmer sauce of your choice (see page xv)

1. Scrub the potatoes and microwave until done. Start with 2 minutes per potato, then add time as needed. They should be fairly soft, but not collapsed.

2. Meanwhile, rinse the greens and wilt down in a large skillet or stir-fry pan. Drain well.

3. Return the greens to the pan along with the scallions and cilantro. Stir in enough of the Indian simmer sauce to be generous without drowning the greens. Cook briefly over medium heat until the mixture comes to a gentle simmer.

4. Cut the cooked potatoes in half lengthwise and smash lightly with a large fork. Divide the greens among them and serve at once.

NOTE
You'll find power greens shelved near baby spinach and other packaged greens. If you can't find it, use baby spinach. This dish will taste just as good!

SMASHED POTATOES
WITH MUSHROOM GRAVY

Few dishes are more comforting than mashed potatoes with gravy, but what seems like a simple preparation is a bit of a project with a fair amount of peeling, dicing, and cooking. Smashed potatoes are far easier to accomplish. No need to save this classic just for special occasions!

4 SERVINGS

4 large golden or russet potatoes

8 to 10 ounces cremini mushrooms, cleaned and sliced

1½ cups vegetable broth

2 tablespoons unbleached white flour

¼ cup nutritional yeast

¼ teaspoon salt, or to taste

Freshly ground pepper, to taste

1. Scrub the potatoes and microwave until done. Start with 2 minutes per potato, then add time as needed. They should be fairly soft, but not collapsed.

2. Combine the mushrooms with about ¼ cup of the broth in a medium saucepan. Cook over medium heat until wilted down, about 5 minutes.

3. Meanwhile, cut the cooked potatoes in half lengthwise and smash lightly with a large fork.

4. In a small cup, stir together the flour and enough of the remaining broth to make a smooth and flowing gravy thickener. Slowly whisk it into the mushroom mixture in the saucepan, then whisk in the remaining broth and nutritional yeast.

5. Bring the mixture to a simmer, and cook briefly until thickened. Season the gravy with salt and pepper.

6. Distribute the gravy over the smashed potatoes and serve at once.

OPTIONAL ADDITION

✳ Add some color with finely chopped fresh parsley or a few sprigs of thyme or oregano.

SMASHED PIZZA POTATOES

Marinara sauce, melted vegan cheese, and steamed vegetables on a potato add up to an irresistible pizza-flavored vegetable dish. Potatoes make for a healthy "crust" that's low in fat and naturally gluten-free. The kids will love this! Vary the vegetable toppings as you'd like. Try peppers, onions, artichokes, and other favorite pizza veggies. For a complete meal, just add a green salad with some chickpeas or beans tossed in.

4 SERVINGS

4 large baking potatoes (Russet works well)

2 to 3 cups finely chopped broccoli (or see Variations)

1½ to 2 cups cleaned, sliced, and stemmed brown or white mushrooms

2 cups marinara or pizza sauce, or as needed

1½ to 2 cups grated mozzarella-style nondairy cheese

1. Scrub the potatoes and microwave until done. Start with 2 minutes per potato, then add time as needed. They should be fairly soft, but not collapsed.

2. Cut the cooked potatoes in half lengthwise and smash lightly with a large fork. Arrange the potato halves on a large platter.

3. Meanwhile, steam the broccoli and mushrooms in a skillet with a small amount of water until just tender, then drain well.

4. Spread each potato half with marinara sauce, followed by a sprinkling of grated cheese and some of the broccoli and mushrooms.

5. Microwave the potatoes briefly, until the cheese is melted. Serve at once, allowing two halves per serving.

OPTIONAL ADDITIONS
Top each pizza potato with a dusting of one or more of the following:

* Dried oregano

* Dried basil

* Dried hot red pepper flakes

VARIATIONS
Use these or other vegetables in any combination as toppings:

* Sautéed onions and/or peppers

* Wilted spinach

MORE TIME / LESS LAZY
To bake the potatoes in the oven, start about an hour before you'll need them. Preheat the oven to 400°F. Line a baking dish with foil. Arrange the potatoes in the dish and cover tightly with more foil. Bake for 40 to 45 minutes, or until the potatoes are easily pierced with a knife.

To melt the cheese, you can return the pizza potatoes to the oven for 8 to 10 minutes, rather than microwaving.

CREAMY SCALLOPED POTATOES

This richly flavored take on scalloped potatoes is an old favorite of mine. Using silken tofu instead of a flour-thickened dairy sauce, it's pure comfort. As a main dish, I love this as a side-by-side vegetable dish with **Garlic-Roasted Brussels Sprouts & Baby Carrots** (page 166). Or, serve as a side dish when you have a larger meal planned.

6 OR MORE SERVINGS

6 large or 8 medium potatoes, preferably red-skinned or Yukon gold

2 tablespoons vegan butter

2 large onions, quartered and thinly sliced

1 (12.3-ounce) container firm silken tofu

½ cup unsweetened nondairy milk

Salt and freshly ground pepper, to taste

1. Bake or microwave the potatoes in their skins until done but still firm. When cool enough to handle, peel, and slice about ¼ inch thick.

2. Preheat the oven to 400°F.

3. Heat the vegan butter in a medium skillet. Add the onions and sauté over medium heat until soft and golden.

4. Process the tofu in a food processor until very smoothly pureed, then drizzle in the nondairy milk with the blade still running and process until combined.

5. Combine the potato slices, onions, and pureed tofu in a large mixing bowl and stir together thoroughly. (Don't worry if the potato slices break apart.) Season with salt and pepper, and stir again.

6. Transfer the mixture to a lightly oiled 1½-quart shallow baking dish. Bake until the top is golden and slightly crusty, about 40 minutes. Let the casserole cool for 5 minutes, then serve.

WAYS TO STUFF SWEET POTATOES

Sweet potatoes are vegetable bliss! Not to diss regular potatoes, but sweet potatoes have them beat in nutrients, especially in vitamin A and C. Though sweet potatoes are super tasty in their own right, stuffing them with other tasty ingredients takes them to a whole new level. You haven't really had the ultimate sweet potato experience until you've had one that's been stuffed with tasty fillings.

I recommend using large sweet potatoes for stuffing. If you're not opposed to microwaving, you can make quick work of this, allowing 3 to 4 minutes per sweet potato. They should be well done, but not mushy.

Otherwise, you'll have to plan ahead if you want to bake them (which can take about 45 minutes at 375°F, wrapped individually in foil).

Microwave the sweet potatoes until soft but not collapsed. Allow 3 minutes per sweet potato; test to see if it can be easily pierced, then add another minute or 2 as needed. When the sweet potatoes are ready, split them in half lengthwise, mash the flesh with a fork, and then fill 'em up. The simple ideas that follow will have you eating and enjoying in no time. The best part—you don't need to follow any recipes, just use the ideas below for inspiration, and invent some of your own.

PESTO & MUSHROOM-STUFFED SWEET POTATOES

With just three ingredients, this is one of those beautiful, blissfully easy vegan dinner ideas that practically makes itself. The combination of briny pesto, smooth sweet potato, and earthy mushrooms somehow amplifies these three already-delicious components. As for prepared vegan pesto sauces, there are more available than ever. Look for them in the pasta aisle or produce section of supermarkets and in natural foods stores. My favorite for this dish is artichoke pesto.

3 SERVINGS

3 large sweet potatoes

8 ounces mushrooms (cremini or white), cleaned, stemmed, and sliced

1 (6- to 8-ounce) jar vegan pesto

1. Microwave the sweet potatoes until soft but not collapsed. Allow 3 minutes per sweet potato; test to see if it can be easily pierced, then add another minute or 2 as needed.

2. Meanwhile, cook the mushrooms in a small skillet with a little water until wilted, about 5 minutes. Drain well.

3. Cut the cooked sweet potatoes in half lengthwise and mash lightly with a fork. Divide the pesto and mushrooms among the sweet potatoes and serve at once

MORE WAYS TO STUFF SWEET POTATOES

* **Chili and cheese:** If you have leftover bean chili this is an ideal way to use up those leftovers, but if not, a natural brand of chili like Amy's® is more than fine. Top each with vegan cheese shreds and some diced avocado and tomato. This is particularly filling, so half of a large sweet potato might be all you can handle.

* **Arugula, olive, and avocado:** Peppery arugula, briny olives, and mellow avocado contrast deliciously with the sweet potato. Just layer some arugula leaves on your cooked sweet potato, followed by a dollop of avocado that's been mashed with a little lemon or lime juice, and a sprinkling of chopped green and/or black olives.

* **Hummus and broccoli:** Tangy hummus is a nice foil for sweet potato. Broccoli pulls the two flavors together. You can use store-bought hummus, of course, but if you're feeling less lazy, you can make your own Homemade Hummus (page 17).

* **Spinach and Thai peanut:** The combination of lots of wilted spinach and peanut sauce is made that much more heavenly when it's perched atop a sweet potato. Simply wilt down a batch of baby spinach, bathe it in a good-quality prepared Thai peanut sauce, and load it onto cooked sweet potato halves. With this option, Coconut Creamed Corn (page 163) is a lovely side-by-side dish.

ZUCCHINI & POLENTA MARINARA

What's even better than a comforting casserole at the end of a long, busy day is one that takes almost no time to prepare. This polenta-based casserole is almost silly-easy! A crowd-pleasing, family-friendly main dish, this requires only minimal hands-on time. It's effortless enough to make on weeknights, yet special enough to serve to company.

4 TO 6 SERVINGS

1 (18-ounce) tube polenta

1 (28-ounce) jar good-quality marinara sauce (see Note)

2 medium zucchini, sliced ¼ inch thick

1½ cups grated mozzarella-style vegan cheese

1. Preheat the oven to 425°F.

2. Cut the polenta into ½-inch-thick slices. Spread the bottom of a shallow round or rectangular 1½-quart baking dish with a little of the marinara sauce, then arrange the polenta slices in a single layer. Arrange the zucchini slices over the polenta, then pour the remaining sauce evenly over them.

3. Sprinkle the surface evenly with the cheese. Cover and bake for 10 minutes, then uncover and bake for 5 to 10 minutes longer, or until the cheese is melted and bubbly. Let stand for 5 minutes, then serve.

NOTE

Use a flavorful variety of marinara sauce like fire-roasted tomato or garlic-mushroom.

OPTIONAL ADDITIONS

* Add thinly sliced wilted mushrooms or wilted and well-drained greens to the zucchini layer.

* Garnish with fresh basil leaves.

COMPLETE THE MEAL

Serve the casserole with a simple green salad or broccoli slaw dressed with bottled or **Basic Vinaigrette** (page 71). **Pineapple Coleslaw** (page 54) is a good salad choice as well. A fresh, crusty whole-grain bread or cooked quinoa rounds the meal out nicely.

BAKED SWEET POTATO FRIES WITH CHIPOTLE MAYONNAISE

Adding a spicy mayonnaise is a terrific way to enjoy low-fat oven "fries." These are a wonderful accompaniment to wraps, sandwiches, vegan burgers, and sloppy joes.

4 SERVINGS

½ cup vegan mayonnaise

½ cup chipotle salsa

3 large sweet potatoes

1 tablespoon olive oil

Salt and freshly ground pepper, to taste

1. Preheat the oven to 425°F.

2. Combine the mayonnaise and salsa in a small serving bowl and stir together. Set aside.

3. Peel the sweet potatoes (or scrub well and leave skins on) and cut them into fry shapes, about ½ inch thick. Combine in a large mixing bowl with the oil and toss well to coat.

4. Transfer the sweet potatoes to a parchment-lined baking sheet. Bake for 25 to 30 minutes, stirring gently every 10 minutes, until the sweet potatoes are crisp and lightly browned.

5. Season lightly with salt and pepper, and serve at once with the spicy mayonnaise.

SWEET & SAVORY ROASTED BUTTERNUT SQUASH

Hints of soy sauce and maple syrup make roasted butternut squash absolutely addictive. This dish is a nice addition to everyday or holiday meals during the cooler months. Since this is a book for busy people, this recipe is prepared with fresh pre-cut butternut squash, often found in the supermarket produce section during the fall and winter. If you want to make this from a fresh whole squash, by all means do. See instructions under More Time / Less Lazy following the recipe.

6 SERVINGS

1 (32-ounce) package fresh pre-cut butternut squash

3 tablespoons maple syrup or agave nectar

1 tablespoon soy sauce or tamari, or to taste

2 tablespoons oil

1½ teaspoons salt-free seasoning blend

¼ cup chopped fresh parsley, a few sliced sage leaves, or the leaves from a sprig of rosemary

1. Preheat the oven to 425°F.

2. Combine the squash chunks in a mixing bowl with all the remaining ingredients, except the fresh herb of your choice, and stir together well. Transfer to a parchment-lined roasting pan and roast for 20 to 25 minutes, or until nicely glazed and starting to brown, stirring once or twice.

3. Stir in the fresh herb of choice, then serve straight from the pan or transfer to a covered serving container.

MORE TIME / LESS LAZY

If you'd like to prepare the squash yourself, here's how:

1. Preheat the oven to 375°F. Cut the squash in half lengthwise. Place the squash halves cut side up in a baking dish, and cover each tightly with foil. Bake until easily pierced with a knife but still firm, about 30 to 40 minutes, depending on the type and size of squash used. If you don't have a knife sharp enough to cut the squashes in half, simply wrap in foil, place them in a casserole dish, and bake until they can be pierced through, but are still firm.

2. When the squashes are cool enough to handle, scoop out and discard the seeds. Peel the squashes and cut into 1-inch chunks. This can be done a day or so ahead of time. Store the baked squash chunks in the refrigerator until needed.

PAIRING SUGGESTIONS

Bean dishes, grain dishes, casseroles, and tortilla specialties. As far as recipes in this book, this is suggested as an accompaniment to **Italian-Style Rice & Peas** (page 136) and **Quinoa with Cauliflower & Cranberries** (page 128).

TWO-POTATO HASH BROWNS

I've always loved hash browns as a comforting weekend breakfast dish, though it's equally welcome as a side dish on the dinner plate. This variation gets a nice veggie boost with sweet potatoes and bell peppers. Microwaving the potatoes ahead of time makes them easier to handle. Of course, you're welcome to pre-bake them in the oven instead, if you're so inclined. Serve as a hearty side dish with tofu scrambles, wraps, and vegan burgers. It's also a great side dish with the two **Sloppy Joe** recipes on pages 175 and 176.

6 SERVINGS

4 medium-large golden or red-skinned potatoes, scrubbed

2 medium sweet potatoes, scrubbed

2 tablespoons olive oil

1 medium onion, finely chopped

1 medium red bell pepper, finely diced

1 teaspoon sweet or smoked paprika, or more, to taste

Salt and freshly ground pepper, to taste

1. Microwave the golden potatoes until done but still firm. Start with 5 minutes total, then add a minute at a time until all are done.

2. Microwave the sweet potatoes until done but still firm. Start with 4 minutes total, then add a minute at a time until done. Sweet potatoes microwave unevenly due to the shape, so make sure not to overcook.

3. When the potatoes and sweet potatoes are done and cool enough to handle, cut them into approximately ½-inch dice.

4. Heat the oil in a large skillet. Add the onion and sauté over medium heat until translucent. Add the bell pepper and continue to sauté until the onion is golden.

5. Add the cooked diced potatoes and continue to sauté, stirring often, until the mixture is hot and golden brown. If it seems dry, add a small amount of water to the skillet. Season with paprika, salt, and pepper. Serve from the skillet.

GREENS WITH POLENTA WEDGES

Garlic, olives, and crisp wedges of polenta do wonders to dress up leafy greens. If you've been slacking off on eating healthy greens, this tasty dish just might inspire you to enjoy them more often. This is especially nice paired with bean dishes.

4 TO 6 SERVINGS

1 (18-ounce) tube polenta

2 tablespoons olive oil

10 to 12 ounces kale or chard (any variety of either)

3 to 4 cloves garlic, finely chopped

1 tablespoon balsamic vinegar

½ cup sliced pitted black olives (any variety)

Salt and freshly ground pepper, to taste

1. Cut the polenta into ½-inch-thick slices. Cut each slice into 4 little wedges.

2. Heat a wide nonstick skillet. Add a drop of the oil and spread it around with a paper towel, reserving the rest. Arrange the polenta wedges in a single layer (if your skillet doesn't hold all of them, cook in batches). Cook over medium heat, about 5 minutes on each side, or until golden and crisp. Transfer to a plate and set aside.

3. Meanwhile, strip the greens away from their stems. If you'd like to use the stems, slice them thinly. Cut the leaves into bite-size pieces and rinse well.

4. In the same skillet used to cook the polenta, heat the remaining oil. Add the garlic and sauté over low heat just until it begins to turn golden.

5. Add the greens and just enough water to keep the skillet moist. Cover and steam for 3 to 5 minutes, or until wilted down and tender but still bright green. Drizzle in the balsamic vinegar and stir quickly to coat the greens.

6. Gently fold the polenta wedges in with the greens along with the olives. Season with salt and pepper, and serve at once.

VARIATIONS

* Use sun-dried tomatoes in place of olives.

* Make this even easier by using packaged power greens or baby spinach.

BRAISED BOK CHOY
WITH SHIITAKE MUSHROOMS

Bok choy and mushrooms are made for each other, as you'll discover in this Asian-inspired side dish. Calcium-rich bok choy is one of the easiest greens to use because you needn't bother with stemming. Try this lovely side dish with Asian-style tofu or noodle dishes or serve over rice.

4 SERVINGS

8 stalks regular bok choy or 4 to 6 baby bok choy

4 to 6 ounces shiitake mushrooms, cleaned, stemmed, and sliced

½ cup vegetable broth or water with ½ vegetable bouillon cube

1 to 2 teaspoons grated fresh or jarred ginger

½ teaspoon cornstarch or arrowroot

Salt and freshly ground pepper, to taste

1. For regular bok choy, slice the stems and chop the green leaves roughly. For baby bok choy, slice through the stems and leaves. Rinse either variety well in a colander.

2. Combine the shiitakes in a pan with the broth or water with bouillon cube. Bring to a gentle simmer and cook until just tender. Stir in the ginger, then add the bok choy and cook for just a minute or two until wilted and heated through. (Bok choy cooks quickly and is best with a little crunch.)

3. Combine the cornstarch with just enough water to dissolve in a cup and stir until smooth. Drizzle into the bok choy mixture and cook until the liquid is thickened. Remove from the heat.

4. Season with salt and pepper, and serve at once in shallow bowls or over a hot cooked grain.

RICED CAULIFLOWER WITH CHICKPEAS & MUSHROOMS

Cauliflower "rice" is a clever way to get more of a nutritious vegetable into your regimen. It's also good for anyone who avoids grain foods, not to mention a sneaky way to disguise vegetables for your picky eaters. This recipe starts with a bag of time-and-mess-saving riced cauliflower, widely available in supermarket frozen vegetable sections.

4 SERVINGS AS A MAIN DISH; 6 OR MORE SERVINGS AS A SIDE DISH

1 tablespoon olive oil

3 scallions, thinly sliced, white and green parts separated

8 ounces mushrooms, cleaned, stemmed, and sliced

1 (16-ounce) bag frozen riced cauliflower, thawed

1 (15-ounce) can chickpeas, drained and rinsed

2 teaspoons salt-free seasoning blend

Salt and freshly ground pepper, to taste

OPTIONAL ADDITIONS

❋ Add 2 to 3 tablespoons nutritional yeast for extra flavor and protein.

❋ Stir in as much chopped fresh parsley or cilantro as you'd like.

1. Heat the oil in a medium skillet or stir-fry pan. Add the white parts of the scallion and sauté over medium heat for a minute or two. Add the mushrooms and continue to sauté until just wilted.

2. Add the riced cauliflower, green parts of the scallions, chickpeas, and seasoning blend. Turn the heat up to medium-high, and cook, stirring often, for 7 to 8 minutes, until hot and turning golden here and there.

3. Season with salt and pepper, and serve.

CHINESE-STYLE RICED CAULIFLOWER

Cauliflower rice makes any classic rice dish lighter and is a fun and tasty way to get an additional serving of vegetables into your daily fare. Serve with Asian-style tofu, tempeh, and seitan dishes, or as a side-by-side dish with **Spicy Walnut Green Beans** (page 164).

4 TO 6 SERVINGS

1 tablespoon safflower or other neutral vegetable oil

1 (16-ounce) bag frozen cauliflower rice, thawed

3 to 4 scallions, thinly sliced, white and green parts separated

1 (8-ounce) bag frozen mixed peas, corn, and carrots, thawed

2 baby bok choy or 4 to 6 stalks regular bok choy, sliced and rinsed

¼ to ½ cup sesame teriyaki marinade, or as needed

Freshly ground pepper, to taste

1. Heat the oil in a stir-fry pan or large skillet. Add the cauliflower rice and white parts of the scallions and stir-fry over high heat for 5 minutes.

2. Stir in the green parts of the scallions, mixed vegetables, and bok choy, and continue to stir-fry for 5 minutes longer, or until the cauliflower rice is touched with golden spots.

3. Drizzle in the teriyaki marinade and stir-fry the mixture for a minute or 2 longer. Season with freshly ground pepper and serve.

VARIATION
* Use 2 cups trimmed fresh snow peas in place of the bok choy.

OPTIONAL ADDITION
* Pass around toasted chopped cashews or peanuts for topping.

ROASTED CURRY
CAULIFLOWER

Curry and lemon add offbeat flavor and vivid color to this roasted cauliflower dish. Serve with pasta and grain dishes as a colorful side dish.

6 SERVINGS AS A SIDE DISH

1 medium head cauliflower, cut into bite-size pieces

1 large red onion, quartered and sliced

2 tablespoons olive or safflower oil

Juice of ½ lemon (about 2 tablespoons)

1½ teaspoons fine-quality curry powder

Chopped fresh cilantro or parsley, as desired

Salt and freshly ground pepper, to taste

1. Preheat the oven to 425°F.

2. Combine the cauliflower and onion in a large mixing bowl.

3. Combine the oil, lemon juice, and curry powder in a small bowl and whisk together. Drizzle over the cauliflower and onion and stir until evenly coated.

4. Transfer the cauliflower mixture to a parchment-lined roasting pan and roast in the oven for 15 minutes. Stir, then roast for 10 to 15 minutes longer, or until the vegetables are touched with brown spots.

5. Transfer to a serving bowl and stir in as much cilantro or parsley as you'd like. Season with salt and pepper, and serve.

OPTIONAL ADDITIONS

Stir in or top the finished cauliflower with any of these:

* Sliced sun-dried tomatoes (¼ to ⅓ cup)
* Raisins, dried cranberries, or dried cherries (about ⅓ cup)
* Toasted pumpkin seeds (¼ to ⅓ cup)

BATTER-FRIED CAULIFLOWER

Enjoy this batter-dipped cauliflower as a side dish or even as a veg-centric appetizer. Fresh cauliflower is sometimes a must, especially for roasting, but this recipe works well with frozen cauliflower, sparing you the time it takes to chop it down into cute little florets.

2 TO 4 SERVINGS

⅓ cup garbanzo (chickpea) flour

½ teaspoon salt-free seasoning blend (like Frontier® or Mrs. Dash®)

Salt and freshly ground pepper, to taste

1 (16-ounce) bag frozen cauliflower florets, thawed

Olive or safflower oil for sautéing

Ketchup, sriracha, or marinara sauce

1. Combine the garbanzo flour with ¼ cup of water, seasoning blend, salt, and a few grindings of pepper. Whisk together until the batter is smoothly blended. Add the cauliflower to the batter and stir together until completely coated.

2. Heat just enough oil to coat the bottom of a wide non-stick skillet. Add the cauliflower in a single layer (in batches if necessary) and sauté over medium-high heat, stirring often, until golden brown on most sides.

3. Serve hot or at room temperature with the condiment of choice.

PAN-ROASTED CAULIFLOWER WITH DRIED TOMATOES

If cauliflower is a favorite vegetable, you'll love this way to embellish it with sun-dried tomatoes and crunchy seeds. It's a fantastic side dish that goes with almost anything!

6 SERVINGS

1 medium or large head cauliflower, cut into bite-size pieces

1 tablespoon extra-virgin olive oil

½ cup sliced sun-dried tomatoes (see Note)

Salt and freshly ground pepper, to taste

¼ cup chopped fresh parsley

1. Combine the cauliflower with ½ cup of water in a large skillet or stir-fry pan. Cover and steam over medium heat until tender-crisp, 6 to 8 minutes.

2. Drain out any water from the pan, then drizzle in the olive oil. Turn up the heat and cook, stirring often, until the cauliflower is touched with brown spots.

3. Stir in the dried tomatoes and cook for a minute or two longer.

4. Season with salt and pepper. Sprinkle fresh parsley on top, then serve from the pan.

NOTE
If using dried tomatoes not packed in oil, make sure they're nice and moist. If not, rehydrate in a little hot water before using. If using oil-packed tomatoes, eliminate the olive oil and use a bit of their oil instead in step 2.

OPTIONAL ADDITION
* For extra flavor and crunch, sprinkle some toasted pumpkin or sunflower seeds on top of the dish before serving, or pass them around for topping.

LESS TIME / EVEN LAZIER
Though it won't be as good, feel free to use a completely thawed 16-ounce bag of cauliflower florets in place of fresh cauliflower.

STIR-FRIED COLLARDS & CARROTS

Collard greens, with their imposing leaves, might not be your first choice of vegetable on a busy weeknight. But they deserve a place in your rotation as a source of calcium for the vegan diet—and a tasty one at that. As you'll see, collard greens needn't be cooked to death, as they often are in traditional recipes. This quick stir-fry makes collards much more appealing.

4 TO 6 SERVINGS

1 (10- to 12-ounce) bunch collard greens

1½ tablespoons olive oil

1 medium onion, finely chopped, or 1 whole shallot, chopped

2 to 3 cloves garlic, minced

1½ cups pre-grated carrots or thin baby carrots

1 tablespoon lemon juice

Salt and freshly ground pepper, to taste

1. Cut the collard green leaves away from their stems with a sharp knife or kitchen shears. Stack 6 to 8 similar-size leaf halves on top of one another. Roll up tightly from one of the narrow ends, then slice thinly crosswise. Chop the slices in a few places to shorten the ribbons. Repeat with the remaining leaves. Place in a colander and rinse well.

2. Heat the oil in a skillet or stir-fry pan. Add the onion and sauté over medium heat until translucent. Add the garlic and continue to sauté until the onion is golden.

3. Add the collard greens and carrots. Turn up the heat to medium-high and cook, stirring often, about 4 to 5 minutes, or until the collards are bright green and tender-crisp. Add tiny amounts of water as needed to moisten the pan.

4. Drizzle in the lemon juice and season with salt and pepper. Serve at once.

STIR-FRIED GREENS & NAPA CABBAGE

Even a bunch of greens can cook down to a small quantity. In this flavorful side dish, napa cabbage not only stretches them out, but is the perfect cruciferous companion. It lightens the texture and adds eye appeal as well.

4 TO 6 SERVINGS

10 to 12 ounces kale or chard, stemmed and thinly sliced

½ medium head napa cabbage

2 tablespoons olive oil

1 medium onion, finely chopped

2 to 4 cloves garlic, minced

Salt and freshly ground pepper, to taste

1. Cut the kale or chard leaves away from the stems. If you'd like to use the stems, slice them thinly. Cut the leaves into ribbons and rinse well.

2. Cut the napa cabbage into ribbons.

3. Heat the oil in a stir-fry pan. Add the onion and sauté over medium heat until golden. Add the garlic and continue to sauté over medium-low heat until the onion is golden.

4. Stir in the greens, then turn the heat up to high and stir-fry 2 minutes or so. Add the napa cabbage and continue to stir-fry until both the greens and cabbage are tender-crisp, about 2 to 3 minutes longer. Season with salt and pepper, and serve at once.

OPTIONAL ADDITIONS

* A sprinkling of sesame seeds is highly recommended. This looks especially nice with black sesame seeds.

* Add a fresh hot chile pepper to the stir-fry or dried hot red pepper flakes, to taste, at the end.

TAHINI-LEMON GREENS

There's something about tahini (sesame paste) that's incredibly compatible with greens. This dish provides a double dose of plant-based calcium from the greens and tahini, but it's the flavor that will win you over. This is e8specially good as a companion to grain dishes.

4 SERVINGS

Large bunch (about 12 ounces) fresh greens (kale, collards, or chard)

1 to 2 tablespoons olive oil

3 to 4 cloves garlic, crushed

⅓ cup tahini (sesame paste)

Juice of 1 to 1½ lemons

1 tablespoon agave nectar or maple syrup

Salt and freshly ground pepper, to taste

1. Cut the leaves of the greens away from the stems. If you'd like to use the stems from the kale or chard, slice them thinly; stems from the collards should be discarded. Chop the leaves of the kale or chard into bite-size pieces. For collard greens, stack 6 to 8 similar-size leaf halves on top of one another at a time and roll up tightly from one of the narrow ends, then slice thinly crosswise. Chop the slices in a few places to shorten the ribbons. Whatever kind of greens you're using, rinse well in a colander.

2. Heat the oil in a large steep-sided skillet or stir-fry pan. Add the garlic and sauté over low heat for 2 to 3 minutes, until golden. Add the greens and cook over medium heat, stirring often until just tender and still bright green, about 5 to 7 minutes. Add small amounts of water if needed, just enough to keep the bottom of the pan moist. Remove from the heat.

3. Combine the tahini, lemon juice, and agave in a small bowl and whisk together. Stir into the greens until evenly coated. Season with salt and pepper, and serve at once.

COCONUT CREAMED CORN

This side dish is a wonderful way to use fresh corn while it's still abundant, but after the novelty of eating it on the cob has worn off. The most time-consuming part of this is stripping the corn kernels off the cob, and that takes all of 5 minutes.

4 SERVINGS

4 ears fresh corn

3 scallions, sliced, white and green parts separated

1 cup light coconut milk

⅓ cup chopped fresh cilantro leaves, or to taste

½ medium red bell pepper, finely diced

Salt and freshly ground pepper, to taste

1. Break each ear of corn in half, stand it on its flat end, and cut the kernels off the cob with a small, sharp knife.

2. Combine the corn kernels, white parts of the scallion, and coconut milk in a skillet. Bring to a gentle simmer over medium heat, then cook for 2 to 3 minutes, or until the corn kernels are tender-crisp.

3. Stir in the green parts of the scallion, cilantro, and bell pepper. Remove from the heat and season with salt and pepper. Serve warm or at room temperature.

OPTIONAL ADDITIONS

＊ Spice the dish up with one or two fresh hot chile peppers (seeded and minced) or dried hot red pepper flakes, to taste.

SPICY WALNUT GREEN BEANS

Crunchy green beans in a rich, nutty coating of walnuts and lots of garlic go well with tofu, tempeh, and grain entrées as a side dish. This can also be served as a room-temperature appetizer.

6 SERVINGS

12 to 16 ounces green beans, trimmed (or use frozen whole green beans)

5 to 6 cloves garlic, minced

⅓ cup sweet chili sauce

⅓ cup finely chopped walnuts

Dried hot red pepper flakes, sriracha, or other hot seasoning, to taste

1. Combine the green beans and garlic with about ½ cup of water in a stir-fry pan. Steam over medium-high heat, covered, for 5 minutes. Drain the water from the pan.

2. Stir in the chili sauce and turn up the heat to high. Stir-fry until the green beans are tender-crisp and touched with brown spots.

3. Add the walnuts, followed by the hot seasoning, to taste, and toss together. Or, you can just pass the hot stuff around for everyone to spice up their own serving.

4. Remove from the heat and transfer to a serving platter. Serve warm or at room temperature.

HOISIN-GLAZED EGGPLANT

Here's a simple way to prepare the abundance of Japanese eggplants or mini eggplants of summer. A hoisin and wine sauce is absorbed by the small eggplants, making them irresistible. Serve with Asian-style tofu or noodle dishes. This also makes a nice room-temperature appetizer.

4 SERVINGS

- **4 long Japanese eggplants or 4 mini eggplants**
- **¼ cup hoisin sauce**
- **¼ cup dry white wine**
- **1 tablespoon soy sauce or tamari**
- **1 to 2 scallions, thinly sliced, for garnish**

1. Trim the stems off the eggplants and discard; cut the eggplants in half lengthwise.

2. Whisk together the hoisin sauce, wine, and soy sauce in a small bowl. Pour the mixture into a large, wide skillet and heat over medium heat until the mixture starts bubbling.

3. Arrange the eggplant halves, cut sides down, in the skillet. Cook for 8 minutes over medium heat, moving them around so that they can absorb more of the marinade in the pan. Turn the heat up and cook for 3 to 4 minutes longer, or until the eggplant is tender but not overdone.

4. Arrange the eggplant halves, cut sides up, on a platter. Sprinkle evenly with the scallion slices. Serve warm or at room temperature.

OPTIONAL ADDITIONS
* Sesame or hemp seeds for garnish

GARLIC-ROASTED BRUSSELS SPROUTS & BABY CARROTS

Brussels sprouts, once the pariah of the vegetable world, are now the cool kids on the block. That happened when roasting them came along, bringing out their best qualities. The tedious thing about Brussels sprouts is that they require a fair amount of prep, and the nice thing about baby carrots is that they require no prep—so combining the two balances things out. This recipe makes a generous quantity, so it's an ideal side dish to make and share for special occasions like Thanksgiving. As suggested in the headnote for Creamy Scalloped Potatoes (page 143), these two vegetable dishes pair well (and can bake in the same oven).

6 SERVINGS

1 pound baby carrots (preferably more slender than chunky)

1 pint Brussels sprouts (or about 2 heaping cups), trimmed and quartered

1½ tablespoons olive oil

3 to 4 cloves garlic, minced

Several sprigs fresh thyme or ½ teaspoon dried

Salt and freshly ground pepper, to taste

1. Heat the oven to 400°F.

2. Combine the carrots and Brussels sprouts in a parchment-lined roasting pan, drizzle the oil over them, and stir to coat. Bake for 15 minutes. Remove the pan from the oven and stir in the garlic. Roast for 10 to 15 minutes longer, or until the vegetables are just crisp-tender and touched with brown spots.

3. Remove the pan from the oven and stir in the thyme. Season with salt and pepper, then transfer to a serving platter. Serve at once.

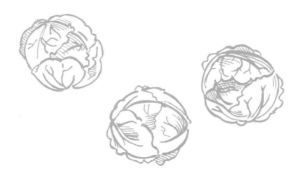

SPICY SESAME BROCCOLI

There's no such thing as too much broccoli, a favorite year-round green vegetable. Sriracha or red pepper flakes give this speedy side dish a spark of heat, and sesame seeds add a subtle crunch.

4 SERVINGS

2 large or 3 medium broccoli crowns

1 tablespoon safflower or other neutral oil

1 tablespoon soy sauce or tamari

1 tablespoon natural granulated sugar

1 tablespoon sesame seeds

Sriracha or dried hot red pepper flakes, to taste

1. Cut the broccoli crowns into bite-size florets.

2. Gently heat the oil, soy sauce, sugar, and about 2 tablespoons of water in a stir-fry pan or large skillet. Add the broccoli and stir quickly to coat. Turn the heat up to high and stir-fry until the broccoli is bright green and just tender-crisp.

3. Stir in the sesame seeds, season with sriracha, and serve.

8

WRAPS & SANDWICHES

This collection of streamlined **WRAPS, SANDWICHES,** and **SANDWICH-Y** things, like **SLOPPY JOES** and **QUESADILLAS,** aims to bring you some fresh ideas for **QUICK** and **DELICIOUS** meals. After all, sandwich fare never goes out of fashion for lunch or dinner, especially when time is tight. And, for those who want to cut back on carbs, wraps provide a nice alternative to bread. I've long maintained that many kinds of **WRAPS ARE REALLY SALADS** in disguise.

These recipes might also **SHAKE UP YOUR ROUTINE** when it comes to portable lunches for work or school. The nice thing about sandwich-type recipes is that **THEY'RE MEANT TO SPARK INSPIRATION,** rather than to be followed slavishly. And, whenever you have a bit more time and you're looking to add a lively soup or salad accompaniment, suggested pairings are offered throughout the chapter.

PESTO OR HUMMUS FLATBREADS

These fun little flatbreads are a nice change of pace from pizza. All you need to do is crisp up store-bought flatbreads in a hot skillet and you are ready to add your own luscious toppings.

Choose flatbreads no larger than about 8 inches in diameter so they can fit in a standard skillet. You can use small partially-baked pizza crusts, sturdy pita breads, or even Indian breads.

4 SERVINGS

4 flatbreads (mini pizza crusts, pita, naan, etc.)

1 cup hummus or vegan pesto, or as needed

Two big handfuls of baby arugula or spinach leaves, or as needed

½ pint cherry or grape tomatoes, sliced

½ cup pitted black olives, sliced

1. Heat a medium-size skillet. Grill one flatbread at a time over medium heat, until golden brown on both sides.

2. Remove from the heat and spread the flatbread with about ¼ cup of hummus or pesto, or enough to cover generously. Cut into quarters and sprinkle with some of the arugula, cherry tomatoes, and olives. Repeat with the remaining flatbreads.

MORE TIME / LESS LAZY
Make your own Homemade Hummus (page 17) or Pesto (page 99).

"TOFUNA" SANDWICH SPREAD

This sandwich spread is one of my standards, and quite possibly the recipe I make most often. If I'm having guests for lunch or brunch, I often make a batch of this no matter what else I'm serving, and it practically gets inhaled. Use this as a spread for sandwiches—closed or open-faced—or just enjoy on its own on the plate or mounded over greens. Though all you absolutely need are three ingredients, the two optional ingredients are highly recommended.

4 TO 6 SERVINGS

1 (8-ounce) package baked tofu (see Note)

½ cup vegan mayonnaise, or as desired

1 large celery stalk, finely diced

1. Using your hands, crumble the tofu finely into a mixing bowl. Or, break the tofu into a few pieces, place in a food processor, and pulse on and off until finely and evenly chopped, then transfer to a mixing bowl.

2. Add the mayonnaise and celery. Mix thoroughly. Transfer to a smaller serving container or serve straight from the mixing bowl.

OPTIONAL ADDITIONS

✳ 1 scallion (green part only), thinly sliced

✳ 2 tablespoons nutritional yeast

NOTE
Soyboy® Tofu Lin or Soyboy smoked flavor are my favorite varieties of baked tofu for this recipe.

WAYS TO MAKE VEGAN
GRILLED CHEESE SANDWICHES

Grilled cheese has become really hot, so to speak. There are even restaurants devoted solely to the theme. It may be far from a super-nutritious food, but a grilled cheese sandwich hits the spot when you're looking for comfort in a hurry. And the add-ins suggested here take them from nursery food to more adult fare.

Seriously, you don't need a formal recipe to make grilled cheese sandwiches, just some sturdy whole-grain bread, vegan cheese, your add-ins of choice, and vegan butter or olive oil. Here are five tasty ways to make this classic sandwich, vegan style:

1 **GRILLED CHEESE WITH TOMATO AND VEGAN BACON:** Use your favorite brand of vegan bacon. Or, when you have more time, make **Sweet and Smoky Tempeh Strips** (page 92). Lightly oil a pan, then cook as much vegan bacon as needed (3 to 4 strips per sandwich) until lightly browned on both sides. Remove from the pan.

Layer on a slice of bread: vegan cheese shreds, tomato slices, bacon, and more cheese shreds. Top with another slice of bread. In the same pan, cook the sandwich in a little vegan butter or olive oil over medium heat, covered, until both sides are golden. This is good with cheddar, mozzarella, or pepper jack.

2 **GRILLED CHEESE WITH BROWN MUSHROOMS:** Clean, stem, and slice brown mushrooms like cremini or shiitake. In the pan you'll be using for the grilled cheese, cook the mushrooms until wilted, then remove from the pan and drain. Wipe out the pan.

Layer on a slice of bread: cheese shreds, cooked mushrooms, more cheese shreds, and another slice of bread. Cook in a little vegan butter or olive oil over medium heat, covered, until both sides are golden. I think this is best with mozzarella-style vegan cheese, but use whatever you've got on hand.

3 **GRILLED CHEESE WITH JALAPEÑO:** Spice up your grilled cheese with fresh jalapeño! Remove seeds and thinly slice a jalapeño or two, depending on how many sandwiches you're making. Or, you can use sliced jalapeños from a jar.

Layer on a slice of bread: cheese shreds, sliced jalapeños, more cheese shreds, and another slice of bread. Cook in a little vegan butter or olive oil over medium heat, covered, until both sides are golden. I like this with a combination of cheddar and mozzarella-style vegan cheese shreds, but either one works well.

4 **GRILLED CHEESE WITH APPLE:** Apple and cheddar are a classic flavor duo, and they harmonize well in a vegan grilled cheese. Using a tart Granny Smith apple is my first choice, but if you've got a sweet red apple on hand, go for it, as long as it's crisp and juicy.

Layer on a slice of bread: vegan cheddar cheese shreds, apple slices, more cheese shreds, and another slice of bread. Cook in a little vegan butter or olive oil over medium heat, covered, until both sides are golden.

5 **GRILLED CHEESE WITH WILTED SPINACH OR ARUGULA:** A vegan grilled cheese sandwich with the green goodness of wilted spinach or arugula is sublime. My first choice for this would be baby arugula. For each sandwich, use a big handful of baby arugula or spinach. I always like to rinse greens even if they're triple-washed. Wilt the greens in a pan with just the water clinging to the leaves. Transfer to a colander and squeeze out the liquid. Wipe out the pan.

Layer on bread: cheese shreds, wilted greens, more cheese shreds, and another slice of bread. Cook in a little vegan butter or olive oil over medium heat, covered, until both sides are golden. Any kind of vegan cheese works well here; for a spicy kick, try pepper jack.

ITALIAN MEATBALL SUBS

Familiar and hearty, these Italian meatball subs are made with a sneaky hack. Using vegan burgers is a clever way to make these tasty bites almost instantly. Use a vegan burger that's based on grains and beans, rather than processed soy. There are many flavorful options available that are based on quinoa, black beans, kale, oats, and other whole ingredients. My favorite for making these instant meatballs is Amy's® California Burger.

Since these subs skew toward bread-y comfort, make sure to add plenty of vegetables to the plate. Steamed fresh asparagus, green beans, or broccoli and any kind of slaw (for some ideas, see pages 52 to 57) add little work to the meal and go nicely with the sub.

4 SERVINGS

1 (4-pack) vegan burgers (your favorite brand)

Olive or vegetable oil or cooking oil spray for the skillet

2 cups marinara sauce (your favorite variety), more or less, as needed

4 hero rolls, preferably whole-grain

1 to 1½ cups vegan mozzarella cheese shreds

1. Cut each burger into four equal quarters. With damp hands, form the quarters into balls. You'll wind up with 16.

2. Lightly coat a nonstick skillet with oil or cooking oil spray. Sauté the meatballs over medium heat, turning gently and frequently, until lightly browned on most sides. (Or bake them in a 350°F oven or toaster oven for 15 to 20 minutes, turning them halfway through.) When done, remove from the skillet to a covered dish.

3. Slather some marinara sauce on both cut sides of a split-open hero roll. Arrange 4 meatballs inside, then sprinkle in a little of the mozzarella cheese shreds.

4. Microwave the finished heroes until the cheese melts, but don't overdo it—30 to 40 seconds should do. Or, if you have the oven on, pop them in there for no more than 10 minutes.

CRAZY-EASY SLOPPY JOES

There are 101 great ways to use vegan burgers beyond just burgers, including the one for Italian Meatball Subs (page 174). Many packaged burger crumbles and meat imitators are based on soy protein isolate, perhaps not the healthiest ingredient. Vegan burgers, on the other hand, offer a wider range of ingredients, including quinoa, beans, kale, pea protein, and more.

In these ridiculously easy sloppy joes, vegan burgers and a jar of salsa give you lots of flavor with little effort. It's an emergency dinner that tastes like anything but. All you need to complete a meal is fresh corn on the cob and a simple salad or slaw.

3 TO 4 SERVINGS

1 (4-pack) vegan burgers

Olive or safflower oil

1 (16-ounce) jar salsa (any chunky variety works; black bean and corn is great here)

2 teaspoons chili powder, more or less, to taste

1 package whole-grain English muffins or burger buns

2 to 3 scallions, thinly sliced

1. Crumble up the veggie burgers. Heat a little oil in a skillet and add the crumbled burgers and the salsa. Add the chili powder and cook over medium heat until the mixture is piping hot and starting to brown, about 8 minutes.

2. If using you're English muffins, split one per person and toast the halves. If you're using burger buns, split them, but there's no need to toast, unless you prefer to.

3. For each serving, arrange two halves of English muffin or burger bun on individual plates. Ladle some sloppy joe filling on each, and garnish with a sprinkling of sliced scallion.

LENTIL
SLOPPY JOES

With a double dose of barbecue flavors, lentils are transformed into tasty high-protein sloppiness on a bun. A simple vegetable side dish, salad, or slaw completes a nearly-instant meal.

4 TO 6 SERVINGS

1 tablespoon olive oil

1 medium onion, finely chopped

2 (15-ounce) cans brown lentils, drained and rinsed

1½ cups barbecue sauce (your favorite variety)

1 tablespoon barbecue seasoning (like mesquite or smoky maple), or chili powder

Whole-grain hamburger buns or English muffins

1. Heat the oil in a medium skillet. Add the onion and sauté over medium heat until golden. Add the lentils, barbecue sauce, and seasoning to the skillet and stir together. Bring to a gentle simmer, then reduce the heat and cook for 5 to 8 minutes, until piping hot.

2. Serve over open-face hamburger buns or split and toasted English muffin halves.

TOFU, ARUGULA & OLIVE WRAPS

Baby arugula livens up the flavor of wraps featuring baked tofu, crisp cucumber, and olives. The combination of flavors makes them an appealing choice for a portable or at-home lunch. To bulk this up for dinner, make a batch of **Super-Easy Guacamole** (page 22) to be scooped up with stoneground tortilla chips. The recipe doubles easily for four wraps.

MAKES 2 WRAPS

2 large (10- to 12-inch) whole-grain wraps

Vegan mayonnaise, as needed

Baby arugula leaves, as needed

½ (8-ounce) package or one 5.5-ounce package baked tofu (any variety)

½ cup chopped briny black olives

1. Place a wrap on a plate or cutting board. Spread with vegan mayonnaise. Put a big handful of arugula in the center. Arrange a row of baked tofu strips next to it, then a row of olives.

2. Fold two sides of the wrap over the ingredients, and keep the ends tucked in as you roll it up snugly to enclose them. Cut in half with a sharp knife.

3. Repeat with the remaining wrap and serve.

OPTIONAL ADDITIONS

* A drizzle of mustard

* ½ cup crisp cucumber, quartered and thinly sliced

BAKED TOFU & PEANUT SATAY WRAPS

Sometimes, two shortcuts are better than one. Using precut coleslaw and prepared peanut satay sauce makes quick work of these tasty wraps. For a portable lunch, add some fresh fruit. For dinner, add a vegetable side dish or fresh corn on the cob. The recipe doubles easily for four wraps.

MAKES 2 WRAPS

2 cups bagged coleslaw or thinly sliced cabbage

½ cup bottled peanut satay sauce, plus more for wraps

2 large (10- to 12-inch) whole-grain wraps

½ red bell pepper, cut into narrow strips

½ (8-ounce) package or one 5.5-ounce package baked tofu (any variety)

1. Combine the coleslaw with about ½ cup of the satay sauce in a mixing bowl. Toss together until the slaw is evenly coated.

2. Spread more satay sauce almost to the edge of each wrap. Divide the slaw, peppers, and tofu in a row down the center of each.

3. Fold two sides of the wrap over the ingredients, and keep the ends tucked in as you roll it up snugly to enclose the ingredients. Cut in half with a sharp knife.

4. Repeat with the remaining wrap and serve.

WAYS TO MAKE AVOCADO TOAST

Maybe avocado toast isn't quite the hot food trend that it was when it first burst onto the scene. Still, it seems firmly entrenched on casual eatery menus everywhere. With a wealth of healthy fats and carbs, it's perfect for an at-home quick breakfast or lunch or even dinner, too. It's a lovely accompaniment to almost any kind of soup.

Avocado toast may have already turned the corner from trend to modern classic. Here are some ideas to embellish a basic avocado spread, which is beyond fine just on its own! The only exception would be the cocoa and banana variation, a deliciously different take on avocado toast.

BASIC AVOCADO TOAST SPREAD: Start with a ripe, mashable avocado. Cut in half in either direction, get rid of the pit, and scoop the flesh onto a plate. Add a tablespoon or so of lemon juice and mash. Make it smooth or leave a bit of texture, as you prefer. I like to add a tablespoon or so of vegan mayonnaise as well, though that's optional. This makes enough for 3 large or 4 average slices of bread. Enjoy as is, or embellish as follows:

1 **BROWNED MUSHROOMS AND GARLIC:** Cook a clove or two of chopped garlic and some brown mushrooms in a skillet with a bit of water until the mushrooms are wilted, about 5 to 7 minutes. Drain well and top avocado toast.

2 **CHICKPEAS AND SUN-DRIED TOMATOES:** Simply scatter some drained chickpeas and sliced sun-dried tomatoes over the avocado toast.

3 **FRESH HERBS AND RED PEPPER FLAKES:** Chop your favorite herbs and scatter over the avocado toast followed by a sprinkling of hot red pepper flakes. I like to combine sliced scallion and sprigs of dill. Fresh parsley, cilantro, oregano, and thyme are other possibilities.

4 **WILTED SPINACH OR ARUGULA:** Wilt some rinsed baby spinach or arugula in a skillet. Don't overcook! Chop finely and stir into the mashed avocado before spreading on toast.

5 **COCOA-NUT BUTTER:** I call this "not-ella" because it's an all-natural and vegan version of the popular chocolate spread.

Combine 2 teaspoons cocoa or cacao powder, a heaping tablespoon of nut butter, and a tablespoon (or two) of maple or agave syrup with a mashed avocado. Work together with the tines of a fork until completely blended. Spread on toast and top with banana slices if you'd like.

PORTOBELLO & COLESLAW WRAPS

Teriyaki-glazed portobello mushrooms and creamy coleslaw make a dynamic duo in these wraps. They're perfect for an at-home or portable lunch as well as a light dinner served with almost any kind of soup or a vegetable side dish. Like most other wrap recipes, this one doubles easily.

MAKES 2 WRAPS

1 large portobello mushroom cap, cut into ¼-inch-thick slices

2 to 3 tablespoons bottled teriyaki marinade, or as needed

2 cups bagged coleslaw or thinly sliced cabbage

¼ cup vegan mayonnaise, plus more for wraps

2 large (10- to 12-inch) whole-grain wraps

1. Combine the portobello slices with enough teriyaki marinade in a medium skillet to coat generously. Cook over medium heat, stirring often, for 5 to 7 minutes, or until the sauce forms a nice glaze on the mushrooms.

2. Combine the coleslaw with vegan mayonnaise in a mixing bowl and stir until well combined.

3. Spread mayonnaise on the top of each wrap, and arrange some of the slaw and mushroom slices down the center.

4. Fold two sides of the wrap over the ingredients, and keep the ends tucked in as you roll it up snugly to enclose the ingredients. Cut in half with a sharp knife.

5. Repeat with the remaining wrap and serve.

OPTIONAL ADDITIONS

* Add a drizzle of sriracha and/or spicy mustard.

BBQ SEITAN & AVOCADO WRAPS

Barbecue-flavored seitan contrasts delightfully with cool avocado and leafy greens. Like many wraps, this one's a salad disguised as a sandwich. For a portable lunch, accompany with fresh fruit; for dinner, a baked potato or sweet potato is most welcome. Or, go a step further with **Two-Potato Hash Browns** (page 152). You can easily double the recipe for four wraps.

MAKES 2 WRAPS

½ **cup bottled barbecue sauce (your favorite variety)**

8 ounces seitan, finely diced

Two 10- to 12-inch flour wraps

Shredded lettuce or mixed baby greens, as needed

½ **avocado, peeled and thinly sliced**

1. Heat the barbecue sauce in a small skillet. Add the seitan and cook over medium heat until the sauce is reduced and forms a nice glaze on the seitan.

2. Place a wrap on a plate. Put a big handful of lettuce in the center. Arrange a row of seitan in the middle of it, and a row of avocado next to it.

3. Fold two sides of the wrap over the ingredients, and keep the ends tucked in as you roll it up snugly to enclose the ingredients. Cut in half with a sharp knife.

4. Repeat with the remaining wrap and serve.

AVOCADO & SWEET POTATO QUESADILLAS OR SOFT TACOS

The combination of sweet potatoes, avocados, and vegan cheese in soft tacos or quesadillas is downright sensuous. Whether you make these into soft tacos or crispy quesadillas, serve with plenty of napkins! For a bigger crowd or hungrier eaters, double the recipe—these go down easy.

4 SERVINGS

1 large sweet potato

4 soft taco-size (8- to 10-inch) flour tortillas

1 to 1½ cups shredded vegan cheddar or Jack-style cheese

1 medium avocado, peeled, pitted, and thinly sliced

Salsa (your favorite variety; these are great with salsa verde), as needed

1. Bake or microwave the sweet potato in its skin until done but still firm. (To bake, wrap in foil and bake in a 375° F oven for about 45 minutes; to microwave, start with 4 minutes total, then add a minute at a time until done. Sweet potatoes microwave unevenly due to the shape, so make sure not to overcook.) When cool enough to handle, peel and cut into ¼-inch-thick slices.

2. Prepare tortillas or soft tacos on a griddle or large skillet, or in the oven. If you choose the oven, preheat to 400°F.

TO MAKE QUESADILLAS

1. Sprinkle ¼ cup of the cheese on a tortilla. Arrange sweet potato slices over the cheese in a single layer, followed by a single layer of avocado slices. Spoon some salsa over the avocado (enough to flavor and moisten but not to drench). Sprinkle with another ¼ cup of cheese, and cover with another tortilla. Repeat with the remaining tortillas and filling ingredients.

2. To bake, arrange the quesadillas on a parchment-lined baking sheet and bake for 12 to 15 minutes, or until the tortillas turn lightly golden and crisp on the outside.

3. To prepare on the stovetop, heat the quesadillas one at a time on a nonstick griddle over medium-high heat. When the first side is golden and crisp, carefully flip over with a large spatula and cook the other side until golden.

4. Cut each quesadilla into 4 equal wedges, allowing 2 wedges per serving, and eat out of hand.

TO MAKE SOFT TACOS

1. Sprinkle a little of the cheese over one half of each tortilla, then arrange the sweet potato slices over it in a single layer, followed by a layer of avocado, and a dollop of salsa. End with another sprinkling of cheese, then fold the tortilla over.

2. Repeat with the remaining 3 tortillas.

3. To bake, arrange the soft tacos on a parchment-lined baking sheet. Bake for 5 minutes, or just until the cheese is melted well.

4. To prepare on the stovetop, arrange 2 soft tacos on a griddle or large skillet and heat briefly, just long enough to melt the cheese, about 2 minutes per side. Eat at once with a knife and fork or cut each into 2 wedges and eat out of hand.

OPTIONAL ADDITION

* To give these a bit more bite, add slivers of fresh hot chile peppers (jalapeño or serrano) or a drizzle of sriracha sauce to the filling.

SPINACH & BELL PEPPER QUESADILLAS

A slightly sweet salsa and piquant vegan cheese pull together the flavors in these delightful quesadillas. For larger appetites, a whole quesadilla (four wedges) is a good serving; for a lighter meal or if you're serving more with this other than a salad, two wedges can be quite satisfying. These pair nicely with soups and bean dishes.

2 TO 4 SERVINGS

1 medium red or yellow bell pepper, seeded and thinly sliced

5 to 6 ounces baby spinach, rinsed

4 burrito-size tortillas or soft wraps (10 inches or so)

1½ to 2 cups vegan cheese shreds (try pepper jack)

Salsa (try pineapple or mango salsa), as needed

1. Steam the bell peppers in a large non-stick skillet with a little water over medium heat until tender-crisp, about 3 to 4 minutes.

2. Add the spinach, cover, and cook until just wilted down. Drain off any liquid that has formed and transfer from the skillet to a bowl or plate. Wipe the skillet.

3. Lay a tortilla on the surface of the skillet. Sprinkle the entire surface with some shredded cheese. Scatter with some of the bell pepper and spinach mixture, then sprinkle with more cheese, perhaps a little less than the first layer. Cover with another tortilla.

4. Cook over medium heat until the bottom is golden and crisp, then flip with a large spatula and cook on the other side. Transfer to a plate and cover with foil or a pan lid to keep warm.

5. Meanwhile, repeat for the second quesadilla. Once both are cooked, wait about 5 minutes, then cut into quarters.

6. Serve at once, arranging 2 to 4 wedges on each plate.

9

FRUITS
& SWEETS

For the finale, here's a selection of **HEALTHY PLEASURES** that can be made and enjoyed in minutes. Most of these recipes are based on fruits, nuts, seeds, and other whole foods. If you like **DECADENT-TASTING DESSERTS** that can be enjoyed **GUILT-FREE**, you've come to the right place.

In this chapter, you'll find a **DREAMY SAUCE FOR DIPPING** apples or topping ice cream, energy truffles, and a few chocolate-y things. You'll encounter lots and lots of bananas, because one of my favorite sweet treats to make is banana-based "ice cream." Now that you have a stash of guilt-free treats to turn to, you can **INDULGE, LITERALLY, TO YOUR HEART'S CONTENT.**

TWO-INGREDIENT DATE "CARAMEL" SAUCE

The traditional recipe for caramel sauce consists of a cup of sugar, half a cup of butter, and some milk or cream. This amazing sauce, with an almost uncanny resemblance to caramel, is almost the opposite in terms of sugar and fat. Yet, it tastes just as good, and unlike regular caramel sauce, there's no cooking involved. An incredible dip for sliced apples and/or pears, this is also a lovely topping for vegan cakes and ice cream.

MAKES ABOUT 1½ CUPS

1 cup pitted dates (preferably Medjool, but Deglet are fine), plus more as needed

⅔ cup vanilla unsweetened nondairy milk, or as needed

1. Soak the dates in hot water for 30 to 60 minutes, then drain well.

2. Combine the soaked dates and nondairy milk in a blender. Blend until very smooth. If the sauce is too thick to pour out of the blender, add just a touch more nondairy milk and blend again. If the sauce seems thin (it should have body, though it won't be as dense or sticky as sugar-based caramel sauce), add a couple more soaked dates and blend again.

3. Pour into a serving container and serve over nondairy ice cream, vegan brownies, or as a dip with fruit.

OPTIONAL ADDITION

＊ Add a pinch of salt to take it up a subtle flavor notch.

OMEGA-RICH CHOCOLATE FUDGE

Made with hemp seeds and walnuts, this rich-tasting no-bake vegan chocolate fudge is a luscious way to get a nice dose of omega-3 fatty acids.

MAKES 24 TO 36 SQUARES

1½ cups vegan semisweet chocolate chips or chocolate buttons

½ cup natural nut butter (peanut or cashew; make sure it isn't hard and clumpy)

3 tablespoons maple syrup, brown rice syrup, or agave nectar

⅓ cup hemp seeds

¼ cup finely chopped walnuts

TO COOK ON THE STOVETOP:

1. Combine the chocolate chips, nut butter, and syrup in a double boiler or in a bowl perched over a saucepan half-filled with gently boiling water. Cook over low heat, stirring often, until the chocolate is melted. Remove from the heat and stir in the hemp seeds and walnuts.

TO COOK IN THE MICROWAVE:

1. Combine the chocolate chips, nut butter, and syrup in a microwave-safe bowl. Start with 45 seconds, stir, then add 15 seconds at a time until the chocolate is melted. Stir in the hemp seeds and walnuts.

2. Scrape the mixture into an 8 by 8-inch or 9 by 9-inch square baking pan. Smooth evenly, then pat down with the back of a small spatula. Score into 24 or 36 little squares with a butter knife. Refrigerate the fudge, uncovered, for at least an hour to allow it to firm up. (If you're in a hurry, place in the freezer for about 30 minutes.) Serve at once.

3. Store any unused portion in an airtight container in the refrigerator, where it will keep for at least a week.

CHOCOLATE GRANOLA CLUSTERS

Sometimes, when I'm making a fairly elaborate meal for company (and for me, elaborate is a relative term), I lose momentum when it comes to making a dessert. That's when I turn to this clever little no-hassle finale that always gets rave reviews. Imagine, less than ten minutes of prep, no machines, and no baking—just a short time in the fridge to re-solidify the chocolate—and voilà! I serve these bites with pears or apples in the fall, oranges in the winter, strawberries in the spring, and raspberries in the summer.

8 OR MORE SERVINGS

1 cup vegan chocolate chips

2 tablespoons vanilla or plain nondairy milk

1½ cups granola (see Note)

TO COOK ON THE STOVETOP:

1. Combine the chocolate chips and nondairy milk in the top of a double boiler or in a bowl perched over a saucepan half filled with gently boiling water. Cook over very low heat, stirring often, until the chocolate is melted. Remove from the heat and stir in most of the granola, reserving a little for topping.

TO COOK IN THE MICROWAVE:

1. Combine the chocolate chips and nondairy milk in a microwave-safe bowl. Start with 45 seconds, stir, and add 15 seconds at a time until the chocolate is melted. Stir in most of the granola, reserving a little for topping.

2. Line a large plate with wax paper or parchment paper. Spread the chocolate mixture onto it fairly evenly, to a thickness of no more than half an inch. Sprinkle the reserved granola on top. Refrigerate for an hour or so, or until the chocolate has completely solidified.

3. Break the mass into bite-size chunks and arrange on a platter to serve.

4. Store any unused portion in an airtight container in the refrigerator, where it will keep for at least a week.

NOTE

Use a variety of granola that has a nice mixture of oats, seeds, nuts, and dried fruits. It's best to use granola that's fresh and crisp for better texture.

CRUNCHY GRANOLA–PEANUT BUTTER TRUFFLES

Many recipes for "energy balls" require a machine and/or lots of ingredients. These crunchy granola energy balls need neither. Ready-made granola provides several healthy ingredients in one mix (oats, nuts, dried fruits, and sometimes seeds).

MAKES 12 TO 16 TRUFFLES

1¾ cups granola (see Notes)

⅔ cup smooth peanut butter (see Notes)

2 tablespoons maple syrup

Pinch of cinnamon, or to taste

1. Combine the granola (break up any large clumps) with the remaining ingredients and any of the optional additions (see below) in a large bowl and work together using clean hands.

2. With slightly damp hands, form the mixture into 1-inch balls. If things get sticky, dampen your hands as needed.

3. Arrange the truffles on a wax paper or parchment-lined plate and refrigerate for 30 minutes or more to allow them to firm up, then serve at once. (Or, if you can't wait, pop them into the freezer for 10 to 15 minutes.)

4. Store any unused portion in an airtight container in the refrigerator, where it will keep for at least a week.

NOTES

Choose a granola that has a nice mix of oats, nuts, and dried fruits.

It's best to use peanut butter that's not too bottom-of-the-jar stiff, yet not too runny.

OPTIONAL ADDITIONS

Add either or both of these for an extra boost of nutrients:

✳ 1 to 2 tablespoons maca root powder

✳ 1 to 2 tablespoons hemp seeds

CHOCOLATE-NUT BUTTER TRUFFLES

These richly flavored truffles were my kids' favorite homemade snack when they were growing up, and they wouldn't turn them down now, even as young adults. The classic chocolate and peanut butter combo becomes a high-protein snack for kids, teens, and adults alike.

MAKES ABOUT 12 TO 16 TRUFFLES

½ cup natural peanut butter (or your favorite nut butter)

½ cup dairy-free chocolate chips

½ cup raisins or soft apricots

½ cup wheat germ or hemp seeds

1. Combine all the ingredients in a food processor. Process until the mixture is completely smooth. (You may have to stop the machine and reach in with a spoon a couple of times to break up clumps.)

2. Roll the mixture into 1-inch balls and arrange on a plate. Refrigerate for about an hour to allow the truffles to firm up, then serve at once.

3. Store any unused portion in an airtight container in the refrigerator, where it will keep for at least a week.

OPTIONAL ADDITIONS
To create a tasty coating to the finished truffles, roll them in one or more of the following on a small plate before refrigerating:

* Sesame seeds
* Coconut flakes
* Cocoa powder

SEED & NUT BUTTER ENERGY TRUFFLES

An amalgam of tasty and healthful seeds and nut butter, these rich-tasting energy truffles are a nice late-afternoon pick-me-up, post-workout snack, or even a protein-dense treat to start the day. You can vary the nut butters, seeds, and dried fruits each time you make this recipe.

MAKES ABOUT 12 TRUFFLES

½ cup natural peanut, cashew, or almond butter, at room temperature

⅓ cup hemp, sesame, or chia seeds, or as needed

¼ cup sunflower seeds

2 tablespoons maple syrup or agave nectar

¼ cup raisins or dried cranberries

1. Combine all the ingredients except the dried fruit in a small bowl. Work together with the tines of a fork. Depending on the texture of the nut butter, you may need to work in more seeds to firm up the texture. Work the dried fruit into the nut butter mixture.

2. With slightly damp hands, roll into 1-inch balls and arrange on a small plate. Refrigerate for about an hour or so to allow the truffles to firm up, then serve at once.

3. Store any unused portion in an airtight container in the refrigerator, where they'll keep for at least a week.

DRIED FRUIT & WALNUT TRUFFLES

I love healthy treats that the palate mistakes for candy, and these dried fruit and walnut energy balls fit that description. Walnuts are just about the best source of omega-3 fatty acids, a beneficial fat that's not easy to come by in plant-based foods. Eating 3 or 4 of these will give you just about your total daily requirement.

MAKES 12 TO 14 TRUFFLES

1 cup chopped soft dried apricots
or pitted dates

1 heaping cup walnut pieces

2 tablespoons cocoa or cacao powder

1 to 2 tablespoons maple syrup,
to taste

1. If the dried fruit isn't nice and soft, soak it in very hot water for a few minutes, then drain.

2. Put the walnuts in a food processor fitted with a metal blade and pulse until finely chopped.

3. Add the dried fruit, cocoa, and 1 tablespoon of the syrup. Process until the mixture just holds together as a mass (don't overprocess; leave a bit of texture), stopping the machine to scrape down the side of the bowl from time to time. Taste to see if you'd like a sweeter flavor, and if so, add a little more syrup, then pulse a few times to blend.

4. Shape the mixture into balls not more than an inch in diameter. Arrange on a parchment- or wax paper–lined plate and refrigerate for an hour or so to allow the truffles to firm up. Serve at once.

5. Store any unused portion in an airtight container in the refrigerator, where it will keep for at least a week.

OPTIONAL ADDITIONS

* For more energy boosting goodness, add 2 to 3 tablespoons maca powder or hemp seed at the same time as the other ingredients.

* A pinch or a couple of grindings of coarse salt kicks the flavor up. Pulse it into the final food processor mixture, just before forming the truffles.

NUTTY STUFFED DATES

This fabulous no-cook treat was adapted from a recipe by Amy Hemmert and Tammy Pelstring, the original founders of Laptop Lunches (the company that launched a wave of bento-style school lunchboxes). Give this healthy treat of nut-butter and cashew-stuffed dates a try when you need to whip up something quick for your family or guests.

4 TO 6 SERVINGS

12 dates (any type is fine, or try Medjool)

¼ cup cashew or peanut butter, or as needed

24 whole roasted or raw cashews (or 24 halves, if you prefer)

2 tablespoons finely shredded coconut

1. Cut the dates in half lengthwise and remove the seeds (unless they are already pitted). Fill the date halves with cashew or peanut butter.

2. Place a whole cashew (or cashew half) on each filled date. Arrange on a platter and sprinkle with shredded coconut. Serve at once.

3. Store any unused portion in an airtight container in the refrigerator, where it will keep for at least a week.

SKILLET BLUEBERRY CRUMBLE

If you love homemade fruit desserts but aren't much of a baker, you'll appreciate this incredibly easy stovetop skillet crumble. No fruit to pit and cut, no crust to labor over—just a few key ingredients and a perfectly delicious summer finale is ready to serve. Though you can offer the crumble on its own, a scoop of nondairy ice cream makes it something special. Keep this recipe in mind whenever unexpected summer company is coming. It's a lifesaver.

4 SERVINGS

1 pint blueberries, rinsed

2 tablespoons maple syrup or agave, or to taste

1 teaspoon arrowroot or cornstarch, if needed

¾ to 1 cup granola (see Note)

Nondairy ice cream (vanilla or "butter" pecan are best)

1. Place the blueberries in a medium skillet. Cook over medium heat, stirring occasionally, just until they start to burst and become juicy, about 6 to 8 minutes.

2. Add maple syrup to taste. If the mixture becomes too liquidy (which can happen if you leave the berries on the heat for just a few seconds too long), mix arrowroot or cornstarch with just enough water in a cup to form a thickener, drizzle it into the mixture, and cook until the liquid thickens.

3. Transfer the blueberries to a shallow serving bowl, or leave in the skillet. Top with granola as desired. Serve at once over nondairy ice cream.

NOTE
Use a variety of granola that has a nice blend of oats, nuts, and dried fruit.

MORE TIME / LESS LAZY
For added color, cut up a peach, nectarine, or a few strawberries to scatter on top of the berries before adding the granola.

FROZEN BANANA ICE CREAM

Have you discovered banana ice cream? If not, it's high time you did! It's hard to believe that this creamy frozen treat is banana, plain and simple. Simply peel, thinly slice, freeze, and process.

No ice cream machine is needed. All you need is a food processor. (If absolutely necessary, you actually can make this in a regular blender, but it's challenging to get the mixture to blend evenly, and it is difficult to get it out from the bottom of the container. If you only have a high-speed blender don't attempt to use it here. It will liquify the mixture too much.)

Frozen banana ice cream is best made with very ripe bananas. It's a good way to use up overripe ones, too. Slicing the bananas thinly (peeled, of course) before freezing them ensures that it won't be such hard going for your food processor to break them down.

To make frozen banana ice cream look fancier than it really has a right to be, as shown in the photo for **Strawberry-Banana Ice Cream** (page 201), use a pastry piping bag.

BANANA-PEANUT BUTTER ICE CREAM

Banana, peanut butter, and a touch of chocolate are a mighty classic trio that never disappoints. This frozen delight, enjoyed in a bowl or cone, is a healthy treat you won't mind serving your kids—or someone else's kids. Just make sure they leave some for you!

4 TO 6 SERVINGS

4 medium ripe bananas

⅓ cup smooth natural peanut butter

2 tablespoons vanilla nondairy milk, or as needed

¼ cup vegan semisweet chocolate chips

1. Peel the bananas and cut into approximately ¼-inch-thick slices. Place in an airtight container and freeze for several hours or overnight until frozen solid.

2. In a food processor, combine the frozen bananas, peanut butter, and nondairy milk. Process until the bananas are broken down to bits, then stop the machine to scrape down the side of the bowl.

3. Add the chocolate chips and process again until the mixture is smooth and creamy, adding a bit more nondairy milk if needed.

4. Scrape the banana mixture into a container and refreeze for an hour or two, or until firm to the touch. Scoop into individual bowls or cones to serve.

5. Store any unused portion in an airtight container in the freezer, where it will keep for at least a week.

OPTIONAL ADDITION

* Scatter a few roasted peanut halves on top of individual servings.

STRAWBERRY-BANANA ICE CREAM

Vegan frozen strawberry-banana ice cream is made entirely with fruit, making it a treat anyone can enjoy. Scoop it into bowls or serve in waffle cones.

4 TO 6 SERVINGS

4 medium ripe bananas

1 cup sweet ripe strawberries, hulled and halved, plus a few extra for garnish

2 tablespoons vanilla nondairy milk, or as needed

1. Peel the bananas and cut into approximately ¼-inch-thick slices. Place in an airtight container with the strawberries (leaving aside the extras for garnish) and freeze for several hours or overnight until frozen solid.

2. In a food processor, combine the frozen bananas, strawberries, and nondairy milk. Process until the bananas and strawberries are broken down to bits, then stop the machine to scrape down the side of the bowl. Process again until the mixture is completely smooth and creamy, adding a bit more nondairy milk if needed.

3. Scrape the ice cream into a container and refreeze for an hour or two, or until firm to the touch. Scoop into individual bowls or cones to serve. Top with the reserved fresh strawberries.

OPTIONAL ADDITION

* Garnish the ice cream with fresh mint leaves.

MOCHA-BANANA
ICE CREAM

Here's another one that will have you saying "I can't believe it's banana!" The velvety texture and mild chocolate-coffee flavor are sublime.

4 SERVINGS

4 medium ripe bananas

½ cup vegan semisweet chocolate chips

2 teaspoons instant coffee granules

2 tablespoons vanilla nondairy milk, or as needed

Sliced or slivered almonds, for topping

1. Peel the bananas and cut into approximately ¼-inch-thick slices. Place in an airtight container and freeze for several hours or overnight until frozen solid.

2. Combine the chocolate chips, coffee granules, and nondairy milk in a heatproof bowl and microwave for 45 seconds, or until the chips are melted. Whisk until smooth. (Or, you can heat these three ingredients in the top of a double boiler over low heat until the chocolate melts, then whisk together.)

3. Combine the mocha sauce with the frozen bananas in a food processor or blender (if you'd like, save a little of the sauce to use as a topping. Transfer to a small, sturdy plastic food storage bag). Process until the bananas are broken down to bits, then stop the machine to scrape down the sides of the bowl. Process again until the mixture is completely smooth and creamy, adding a bit more nondairy milk if needed.

4. Transfer the mixture to a container and freeze for an hour or two. Scoop into bowls to serve.

5. If you've reserved part of the mocha sauce, snip a tiny piece off one of the bottom corners and drizzle it onto each serving. Add a sprinkling of almonds for topping as well.

PEACH OR NECTARINE & BLUEBERRY ICE POPS

As you may have noticed, recipes for ice pops are popping up everywhere—in food magazines, in the food sections of national newspapers, and on chic summer menus at restaurants around the country, too. Clearly, ice pops are a great summer treat for children of all ages! These refreshing pops call for lush, ripe peaches or nectarines and blueberries, so be patient and wait for the optimal flavor and nutrition that only the best-of-the-season fruits provide. If you like the idea of making ice pops, I encourage you to invest in a set of BPA-free molds.

**MAKES 4 OR MORE ICE POPS,
DEPENDING ON THE SIZE OF MOLDS**

4 to 5 lush, ripe peaches or nectarines, peeled, pitted, and diced

¾ cup mango nectar

1 cup fresh blueberries

2 tablespoons agave nectar or maple syrup, or to taste

1. Combine the peaches or nectarines and the mango nectar in a blender. Blend until perfectly smooth. Turn the motor off. Add the blueberries and stir to combine. Taste to see if the mixture needs a bit more sweetening; if so, add some of the agave nectar to taste.

2. Pour the mixture into ice pop molds and freeze overnight. When you are ready to serve the pops, release them from the molds. If they don't come out of the molds easily, simply let them stand for a few minutes at room temperature, then try again. They should release easily.

CANTALOUPE CREAMSICLE SHAKE

Get a healthy dose of vitamin C and beta-carotene in a smoothie that tastes like an intensely flavored ice cream treat I recall from childhood. This is good enough to serve as dessert and might just become a summer favorite.

2 TO 3 SERVINGS

2 cups diced lush, ripe cantaloupe

1 to 1½ cups orange or carrot-orange juice

1 cup vanilla nondairy ice cream

1. Combine all the ingredients in a food processor or blender and process until smoothly pureed.

2. Adjust consistency with more juice if desired. Serve at once in tall glasses.

BANANA-CHOCOLATE
MOUSSE PIE

Here's one of my golden oldies that never fails to please. Silken tofu is a great base for the smooth mousse-textured filling.

MAKES ONE 9-INCH PIE

2 (12.3-ounce) packages silken tofu

1 cup vegan semisweet chocolate chips

⅓ cup pure maple syrup or agave nectar

1 (9-inch) whole-grain pie crust (try spelt)

2 medium bananas, peeled and thinly sliced

1. Preheat the oven to 350°F.

2. Put the tofu in a food processor or blender. Process until completely smooth. Transfer to a small saucepan.

3. Add the chocolate chips and syrup to the tofu. Cook over medium-low heat, stirring often, until the chocolate chips have melted and the mixture is glossy and smooth. Pour the mixture into the pie crust.

4. Bake the pie for 30 minutes, or until the top of the pudding feels fairly firm to the touch. Allow to cool to room temperature, then refrigerate for at least an hour, preferably two.

5. Just before serving, cover the top of the pie with the banana slices arranged slightly overlapping in concentric circles. Cut into 6 or 8 wedges to serve.

CHOCOLATY BANANA PIZZA

The inspiration for this showy dessert comes from an Italian restaurant in Paris, where it was called "Banana Pizza Chocolatino." My homemade version is just as showy, but it is ridiculously easy. I usually use a neutral-flavored crust for this (not one embellished with herbs, dried tomatoes, etc.), but for a fantastic twist, try a sourdough crust—its slight bite contrasts nicely with the sweet dark chocolate and bananas.

6 SERVINGS

1 good-quality 12- to 14-inch vegan pizza crust

¾ cup vegan dark chocolate chips

2 to 3 medium bananas, as needed, sliced

1 cup sliced, fresh, ripe peeled pear, hulled and sliced strawberries, or whole raspberries

1. Preheat the oven to 425°F.

2. Place the pizza crust on a stone or baking sheet. Cut into 8 wedges.

3. Sprinkle the chocolate chips evenly over the surface of the pizza crust. Bake the pizza for 12 to 15 minutes, or until the crust is golden and the chocolate chips are melted. Remove from the oven.

4. Arrange the fruit evenly over the surface of the pizza, then let the pizza cool for 10 minutes. Serve at once.

CINNAMON SAUTÉED BANANAS

These cinnamon-y chunks of sweet banana offer a warm, homey topping for non-dairy ice cream. But perhaps even more surprising, they are ideal when served as a side dish with spicy or savory dishes. For example, try serving this with **Salsa Black Beans** (page 116) or **Smoky Red Beans** (page 118), all combined atop a rice bowl. For the ideal texture and taste, it's best to use underripe bananas with slightly green peels in this recipe.

4 TO 6 SERVINGS

4 to 6 underripe bananas

1 tablespoon vegan butter, or as needed

Cinnamon, to taste

1. Peel the bananas and cut into ½- to ¾-inch-thick slices.

2. Heat enough vegan butter to coat a wide skillet. When it starts to sizzle, add the sliced bananas and sauté, stirring occasionally, until golden to lightly browned on most sides.

3. Sprinkle in enough cinnamon to coat them lightly and evenly. Serve warm or at room temperature as suggested in the headnote.

PINEAPPLE-ORANGE AMBROSIA

In the winter, when there's a dearth of fresh fruit, this easy, no-cook trio of canned pineapple, oranges, and dried fruit makes a refreshing end to any kind of meal. It makes a nice breakfast dish or simple snack, too.

4 TO 6 SERVINGS

2½ to 3 cups fresh or canned pineapple chunks

4 clementines or other small seedless oranges, peeled and sectioned

½ cup dried cranberries or cherries

1 (6-ounce) container nondairy (coconut or almond) vanilla yogurt

Granola or toasted slivered almonds, for topping

1. Combine all the ingredients except the granola in a serving bowl and stir together.

2. Serve at once in individual dessert bowls, sprinkling each serving with the granola or almonds.

MAPLE-GLAZED PINEAPPLE

Maple syrup makes pineapple even more irresistible, especially when it's glazed right into its surface. This nearly-instant dessert brightens any winter meal.

4 TO 6 SERVINGS

1 tablespoon vegan butter

¼ cup maple syrup

¼ teaspoon cinnamon, or to taste

4 cups fresh pineapple chunks or two 15-ounce cans, drained (save the juice for another use)

⅓ cup dried cranberries, cherries, or blueberries

1. Heat the vegan butter in a medium skillet until melted, then stir in the maple syrup and cinnamon.

2. Add the pineapple to the skillet. Cook over medium-high heat, stirring often, until the pineapple is nicely glazed and beginning to get touched with golden spots, about 6 to 8 minutes.

3. Stir in the dried fruit of your choice and remove from the heat. Transfer the mixture to a serving container, let cool for several minutes, then serve warm.

NO-BAKE STRAWBERRY SHORTCAKES

These sweet little no-bake vegan strawberry shortcakes are made with rounds of prepared polenta in place of baked biscuits. A fun spring or early summer dessert, it's easy enough to make as an everyday treat or for special occasions.

MAKES 6 SHORTCAKES

1 pint strawberries

¼ cup all-fruit strawberry preserves, or as needed

1 (18-ounce) tube polenta

Vegan butter, as needed

1 container vegan whipped cream (see Note)

1. Hull the strawberries and slice very thinly. Cut any large slices in half to make smaller pieces. Reserve 6 small unsliced halves for topping, if desired.

2. Combine the strawberries and enough of the preserves to coat them in a small bowl and set aside.

3. Cut off the puckered ends of the polenta, then cut the rest into 12 equal slices, each about ½ inch thick.

4. Heat enough vegan butter to coat a wide skillet or griddle. Cook the polenta slices in a single layer until golden and slightly crusty, about 7 minutes on each side. If you'd like, replenish with more vegan butter before flipping to the second side. Transfer the polenta slices to a platter and allow to cool to room temperature, or until ready to serve. (If you're impatient and apply the whipped cream to warm polenta, you'll get a runny mess!)

5. When you're ready to serve, layer as follows: a slice of polenta, a small dollop of whipped cream, a few slices of strawberry, another slice of polenta, more whipped cream, a half strawberry (or a few more slices if you didn't reserve halves).

6. Pass around any unused strawberries and more whipped cream to spoon onto individual shortcakes.

OPTIONAL ADDITION

∗ Garnish with small mint leaves.

NOTE

Some brands of vegan whipped cream to look for include So Delicious® CocoWhip! or Soyatoo!® Soy Whip or Rice Whip®.

ACKNOWLEDGMENTS

This will be among the shortest and most heartfelt acknowledgments I've ever written. Many thanks to some of the sweetest people I've ever known and worked with:

My amazing editor and partner in *badinage*, Jennifer Williams

My wonderfully supportive agents, Lisa Ekus and Sally Ekus

My talented food photographers, Evan Atlas (who does double-duty as my son) and Hannah Kaminsky

301 Digital Media, who took over ownership of VegKitchen. com, for permission to reuse food photos from the site

The editors and designers at Sterling Publishing, who always take my work up several notches

PHOTOGRAPHY CREDITS

Evan Atlas: pages 4, 5, 40, 46, 52, 57, 61, 63, 64, 86, 88, 89, 109, 110, 124, 133, 135, 155, 164, 167, 170, 171, 181, 198

Hannah Kaminsky: pages vi, 7, 13, 27, 37, 39, 50, 69, 70, 80, 91, 93, 98, 103, 117, 121, 122, 123, 131, 140, 145, 147, 163, 173, 175, 179, 182, 185, 187, 190, 191, 192, 200, 201, 206, 208, 211

Andrea Skjold Mink: 2; **TopFoodPics:** 16; **Sonelly:** 21; **Indigolotos:** 44; **Shutterstock: Bigio**: 77; **Big Stock: bhofack22:** 151; **GettyImages: dashu83:** 204

Drawings: Nava Atlas

METRIC CONVERSIONS

Get metric equivalents for volume, temperatures, and weights for all of your most commonly used cooking and baking measurements right here.

Volume

US	METRIC
1 teaspoon	5 ml
1 tablespoon	15 ml
¼ cup	60 ml
⅓ cup	80 ml
⅔ cup	160 ml
¾ cups	180 ml
1 cup	240 ml
1 pint	475 ml
1 quart	.95 liter
1 quart plus ¼ cup	1 liter
1 gallon	3.8 liters

Temperature

To convert from Fahrenheit to Celsius: subtract 32, multiply by 5, then divide by 9

FAHRENHEIT	CELSIUS
32° F	0° C
212° F	100° C
250° F	121° C
325° F	163° C
350° F	176° C
375° F	190° C
400° F	205° C
425° F	218° C
450° F	232° C

Weight

US	METRIC
1 ounce	28.3 grams
4 ounces	113 grams
8 ounces	227 grams
12 ounces	340.2 grams

Excerpted from *The Good Housekeeping Cookbook*
(Hearst Books/Sterling Publishing).

INDEX

ABOUT THE AUTHOR

Nava Atlas is the author of many bestselling vegetarian and vegan cookbooks, including *Wild About Greens*, *Vegan Holiday Kitchen*, *Vegan Soups and Hearty Stews for All Seasons*, and many others. Nava also creates visual books on women's issues and runs two websites, The Vegan Atlas (theveganatlas.com) and Literary Ladies Guide (literaryladiesguide.com). She lives in the Hudson Valley region of New York State.

ALSO AVAILABLE BY NAVA ATLAS